JEROME KERN: THE MAN AND HIS MUSIC

WITH HIS WIFE, EVA

Jerome David Kern was born in New York City on January 27, 1885. This date seems significant in the light of the statement above—Kern was born a generation after Victor Herbert and a generation before Richard Rodgers. Factually as well as stylistically, he was the bridge between the old "Viennese" school and the new indigenous "American" one.

His first published song, "At the Casino" was written while he was attending Newark High School in New Jersey. After high school he studied piano, harmony and composition at the New York College of Music and at Heidelburg's famous Conservatory in Germany.

In 1905 he returned home and went to work for T. B. Harms & Co., music publishers. He wanted practical experience and knowledge of the publishing business as well as a chance to make contacts and perhaps work his way closer to his goal: writing for the theater. He became the company's utility man, office boy, piano player and general jack-of-all-jobs. He worked further as a song-plugger at John Wanamaker's department store; when customers wanted to buy sheet music there, he would play tunes for them, like any salesman demonstrating his product.

Kern's first entry into show business came when he was sent to Hammerstein's Victoria Theatre on 42nd Street, in answer to a hurry call for an accompanist by Marie Dressler, then one of vaudeville's leading knock-about comediennes.

But he was more interested in plugging Kern tunes and he soon found out the best way to do it. Oscar Hammerstein II tells us:

He became a rehearsal pianist, and he used this job as a device for selling his own compositions. Here is how it would work: about the third week in rehearsals, when the director, producers and the whole company were pretty tired of the Viennese score they had been rehearsing all that time, Jerry would come back early after lunch and start to tinkle a little tune of his own on the piano. Everyone who came in would say, 'What's that?' 'Oh, just a little thing of my own,' Jerry would answer. Pretty soon everyone thought he had discovered a great potential hit. Jerry's tune had a freshness for them that the over-rehearsed score couldn't possibly have, and the first thing you knew he had interpolated a song into the foreign score!

Kern got songs interpolated into shows with such unlikely titles as MR. WIX OF WICKHAM AND THE RICH MR. HOGGENHEIMER. The songs themselves had pretty unlikely titles, too: "Poker Love," for example, and "Don't You Want a Paper, Dearie?" His first hit was "How'd You Like to Spoon With Me?" from a show called THE EARL AND THE GIRL. That song, incidentally is the first in this collection, written in 1905; Kern was twenty.

For the next ten years, his interpolations were taken thicker and faster, through a welter of oddly-named shows: FASCINATING FLORA, MORALS OF MARCUS, MIND THE PAINT GIRL and A WINSOME WIDOW, to name a few. The "interpolation" part of Kern's career was climaxed in 1914 when he wrote one of his loveliest ballads for Julia Sanderson in THE GIRL FROM UTAH: 'They Didn't Believe Me."

WORKING WITH OTTO HARBACH AT WARNER BROTHERS, 1930

In 1915 Kern formed a collaboration with Guy Bolton and P. G. Wodehouse. Together, the three men turned out a series of musicals often referred to as "The Princess Theatre Shows," the Princess Theatre being where most of them were produced. This was a tiny house—capacity two hundred and fifty—on West Thirty-ninth Street. The Princess Theatre shows had much the same invigorating effect on musical theatre that "The Garrick Gaieties" had nine years later. Both were fresh and even startlingly new in sound and form—and both for the same reason: necessity. As Hammerstein describes The Princess Theatre:

There was no room on the stage for large choruses, and so there were no choruses at all except for ensemble quartets and sextets. A revolutionary orchestra was devised by Kern and his orchestrator, Frank Sadler. A new instrumentation called for eleven musicians because that was about all the pit would hold. These small shows had an intimate quality and a finesse that could not be matched in the larger houses on Broadway, and for many years the three collaborators were the darlings of the critics as well as the Broadway audiences they strove to please.

WITH OSCAR HAMMERSTEIN II AT HIS CALIFORNIA HOME, 1938

Kern's career was now under full steam. In 1915 he was represented in seven productions on Broadway—three of them complete scores. In 1917 and 1918 there were five Kern musicals. One of them, LEAVE IT TO JANE, took him only eight days to write. And not only did the titles of his shows be-

WORKING WITH IRA GERSHWIN ON "COVER GIRL"

come less and less outlandish but the titles of his songs were more familiar. The top of his Broadway career was reached in 1927 with the production of SHOW BOAT. I say "top" because although he wrote four successful Broadway shows afterwards SHOW BOAT is generally considered Kern's best and most popular score. It is the only Broadway score, to my knowledge, to contain as many as five standards: "Bill," "Can't Help Lovin' Dat Man," "Make Believe," "Why Do I Love You?," and "Ol' Man River." (This list excludes "You Are Love," which is only sightly less well known than the others.)

After ROBERTA in 1933, Kern wrote mostly for motion pictures. His last show was VERY WARM FOR MAY in 1939. It was a flop, though "All The Things You Are," the first act ballad, will still be around when many of today's hit shows are long forgotten.

WITH DOROTHY FIELDS AND GEORGE GERSHWIN

In the course of his career, Kern worked with almost sixty collaborators. The lyricists who worked with him most consistently were P. G. Wodehouse, Otto Harbach, Dorothy Fields and Oscar Hammerstein II. According to the latter, Kern was a sharp-tongued, quick-humored man who demanded almost as much from others as from himself. "He could be reasonably tolerant of incompetence, but he could not stand incompetence masquerading as genius," Hammerstein says. "When he met cheapness of any kind he was merciless and shattering."

Vocal affectations also distressed him. Once he was directing an actress who stressed her R's so outrageously that Kern could bear it no longer. When the actress drawled, in her stagy accent, "Tell me, Mr. Kern—you want me to c-r-r-ross the stage, but I'm behind the table. How shall I get ac-r-r-ross?" Kern, gazing at her like an amiable macaw, countered: "Why, my dear, just r-r-roll over your R's!"

In 1945, Kern came East from California not only to attend rehearsals of a revival of SHOW BOAT but also in connection with the score he was about to write, ANNIE OAKLEY, marking his return to Broadway. A few days after his arrival, he collapsed on Park Avenue and was taken to the Welfare Island hospital where he remained in a state of unconsciousness. Hammerstein's description of this is very moving:

He lay unconscious, in the same institution in which Stephen Foster had died. The critical nature of Jerry's condition did not permit his removal to a private hospital. [Kern was moved two days later]. He was in a ward with some fifty or sixty other patients—mental cases, drunks and derelicts for the most part. The doctors had gathered this heterogeneous group together and explained to them slowly and clearly who the new patient was, and asked them to be very quiet and not create the usual disturbances that characterized this room. Not one man disobeyed. The nurse in charge did not go home that night. She extended her duty for that day to twenty-four hours. When Mrs. Kern expressed her gratitude, the nurse answered simply that he had given so much pleasure to her and to the world that she thought she would like to give something to him. It was clear to us all that special consideration and loving care were being granted to this man in a public hospital not because he was wealthy or powerful but because he had devoted almost all his lifetime to giving the world something it needs and knows it needs—beauty.

Jerome Kern died at 1:10 P.M. on November 11, 1945 of a cerebral thrombosis at Doctors Hospital, East End Avenue and Eighty-eighth Street. He was sixty years old.

The songs in this book, selected from over 1,000 songs and 108 complete scores, are divided into two sections: JEROME KERN ON BROADWAY and JEROME KERN IN HOLLYWOOD. They are all in chronological order.

THE LAST KNOWN PICTURE OF KERN. LEFT TO RIGHT, KAY THOMPSON, ROBERT ALTON, LENNIE HAYTON, LUCILLE BREMER, ARTHUR FREED AND KERN.

KERN ON BROADWAY

THE EARL AND THE GIRL. A musical comedy with book by Seymour Hicks, lyrics by Percy Greenbank and music by Ivan Caryll. "How'd You Like To Spoon With Me" lyrics by Edward Laska and music by Jerome David Kern. Produced by Messrs. Shubert at the Casino Theatre on October 27, 1905. 198 Performances. Cast included Eddie Foy, Georgia Caine and Victor Morely.

From the MGM Release "Till The Clouds Roll By," © 1946 Loews, Incorporated

ANGELA LANSBURY SINGING "HOW'D YOU LIKE TO SPOON WITH ME?" IN THE 1946 FILMUSICAL "TILL THE CLOUDS ROLL BY."

Edward Laska reminisces about his collaboration with Kern on his first song hit, in 1905, when the composer was twenty:

I used to hang out at the T. B. Harms offices, and I became acquainted with a chap there who was aspiring to become a composer and he asked me to toss him a lyric sometime . . . One day while I was walking there I conceived a sort of burlesque love song centered around the word SPOON. Reaching the office, I discovered my young friend as usual at the piano and, as usual playing melody after melody into the atmosphere and never bothering to write them down.

"Get this, Jerry," I said — his full name was Jerome David Kern but he dropped the David right after this song's publication [he did continue to use his middle initial] — get this." I gave him the title line and a rough rhythm. At once, as though it were an old song he knew, he played a chorus in the exact length of time it takes to play the chorus now — and it was corking. "Swell," I said. "Now shoot me a verse." And again, the same thing happened!

"How'd You Like To Spoon With Me?" became a "swinging sensation" as the advertisements of the time referred to it. Six girls singing on flower-decorated swings floated from the stage into the audiences of New York's Casino Theatre, and later, in London's Gaiety.

Laska adds an interesting anecdote that was contained in a letter he once received from Jerome Kern's wife, Eva Leale: "She told me how she met Jerry when she was seventeen, and when he mentioned that he had composed 'How'd You Like To Spoon With Me?' she thought he was jesting, for since her childhood she had known it and always thought it was an old English song . . . Sweetly, she added that the little song had been a great part of the beginning of their thirty-five-year romance."

HOW'D YOU LIKE TO SPOON WITH ME

Words by EDWARD LASKA
Music by JEROME KERN

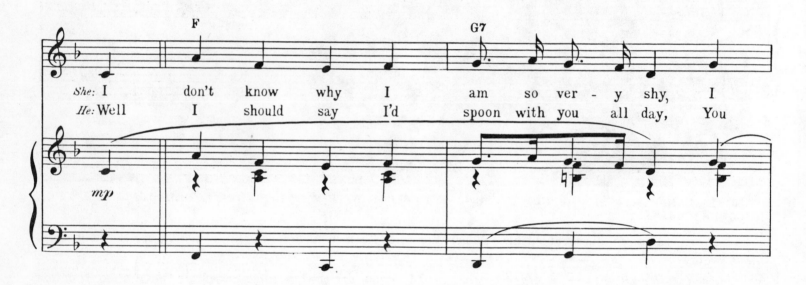

She: I don't know why I am so ver-y shy, I
He: Well I should say I'd spoon with you all day, You

al-ways was de-mure, I nev-er knew what
fas-ci-nate me so, You are so cute, you

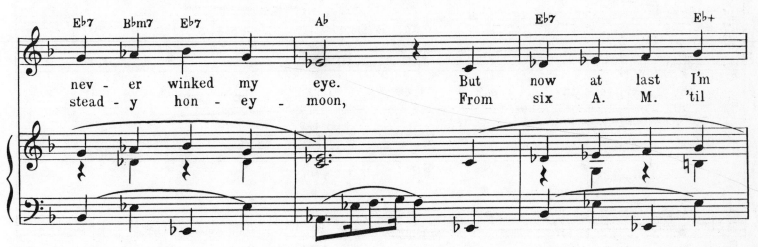

Refrain

She: How'd you like to spoon with me? He: I'd like to

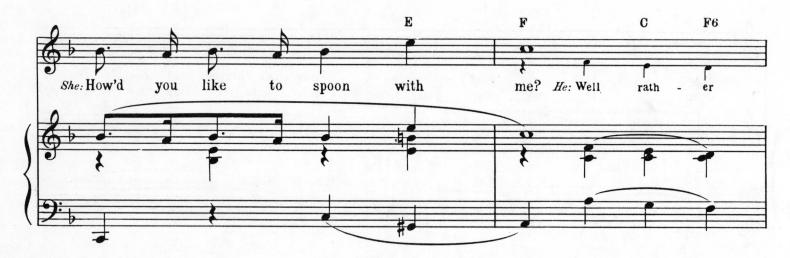

She: How'd you like to spoon with me? He: Well rath - er

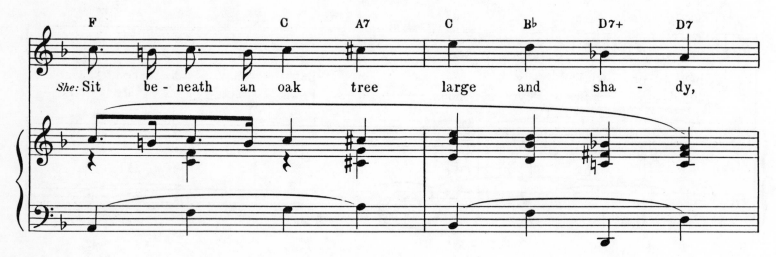

She: Sit be - neath an oak tree large and sha - dy,

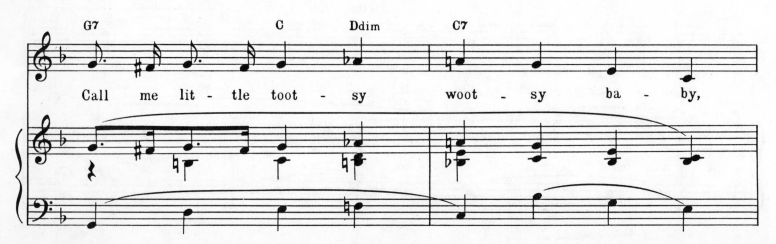

Call me lit - tle toot - sy woot - sy ba - by,

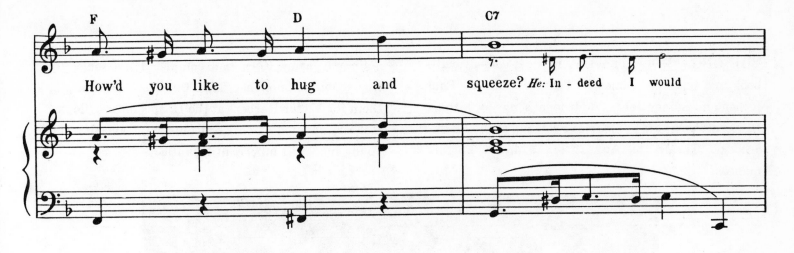

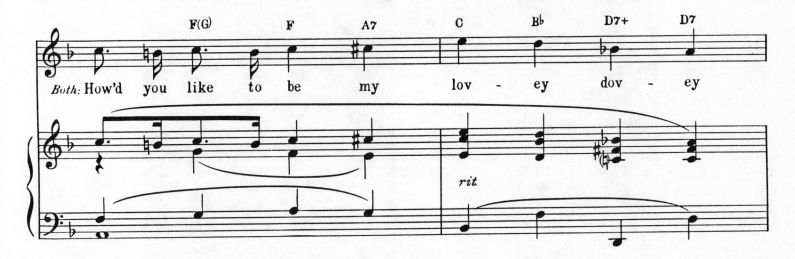

THE GIRL FROM UTAH. A musical comedy with book and lyrics by James F. Tanner. Music by Paul Ruben and Sidney Jones. Additional songs by Jerome D. Kern. Presented by Charles Frohman at the Knickerbocker Theatre on August 24, 1914. 120 Performances.

Shortly after Kern had completed his songs for this show his publisher, Max Dreyfus, had him play them for Victor Herbert at the Harms offices. "Max," Herbert spouted after Kern finished, "someday this young man will inherit my mantle!"

JULIA SANDERSON AND DONALD BRIAN IN "THE GIRL FROM UTAH."

"They Didn't Believe Me" is Kern's first standard and a song that refuses to date because — apart from the easy, fluid melody — the form is still fresh.

The lyric credit is curious — Herbert Reynolds' name as Kern's collaborator appears on this song for the first time. And yet, the ASCAP records indicate that Reynolds and Michael E. (M. E.) Rourke were one and the same person. In any event, Rourke/Reynolds collaborated on many of Kern's songs during the years 1906-1916.

THEY DIDN'T BELIEVE ME

Words by HERBERT REYNOLDS
Music by JEROME KERN

14

Refrain (slowly)

15

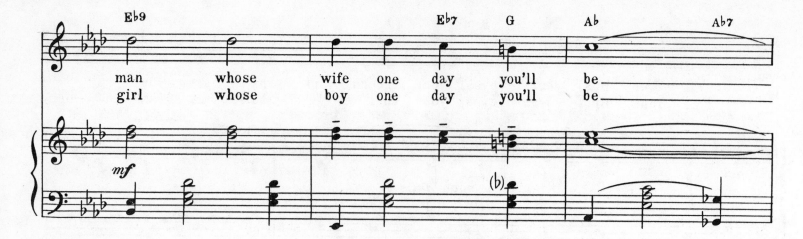

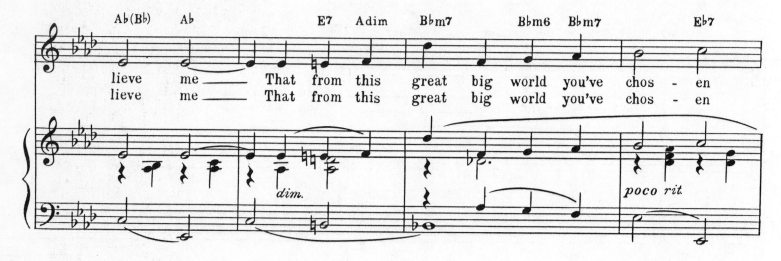

OH BOY! A musical comedy with books and lyrics by Guy bolton and P. G. Wodehouse. Presented by William Elliott and F. Ray Comstock at The Princess Theatre on February 20, 1917. 463 Performances. Staged by Edward Royce. Cast included Tom Powers, Anna Wheaton, Edna Mae Oliver and Marion Davies.

From the point of view of output, the year 1917 was a fabulous one for Jerome Kern. January 11th marked the opening of his HAVE A HEART at the Liberty Theatre, and just four nights later on January 15th, another Kern show, LOVE O' MIKE had its first performance at the Shubert. On February 20th, after a five week hiatus, OH BOY!, his third and most successful of The Princess Theatre shows, was next, with its popular "Till The Clouds Roll By."

Another great hit, LEAVE IT TO JANE, the show that took him eight days to write, came along on August 28th, and the last of the quintet for that year, MISS 1917, opened on November 5th.

Though "MISS 1917" boasted a cast and collaborators among Broadway's most prominent, it closed after only 48 performances and is remembered today mostly for one fascinating aspect—its rehearsal pianist was 19-year old George Gershwin. During rehearsal breaks, Gershwin, who idolized Kern, would entertain the entire company by playing his own improvisations of the score. This whole experience struck a familiar chord with Kern. It was a variation on the same theme—reminiscent of his own tinkering during the early days.

JUSTINE JOHNSTONE (LEFT) AND MARION DAVIES IN "OH BOY."

Aside from being one of many Kern standards "Till The Clouds Roll By" also served as the title for his screen biography. The Metro-Goldwyn-Mayer picture also turned out to be the last project Kern had a hand in.

Arthur Freed, the brilliant musical specialist and a close friend of the composer's took charge of producing TILL THE CLOUDS ROLL BY. On September 6, 1945, when principal photography began, Kern was sitting on the side lines in a supervisory capacity.

Satisfied with the proceedings Kern left for New York on November 4th to attend to other business matters. One week later he was dead. When the news reached Freed at the studio he closed down production. Two months later, with an entirely new screenplay, CLOUDS resumed filming.

For the most part, TILL THE CLOUDS ROLL BY was a fictionalized accounting of Kern's career but he would have wanted it that way. During the early script conferences he remarked: "If it tells the truth, it'll be the dullest picture in the world." In any event, the picture stands as a lasting record of Jerome Kern's genius. TILL THE CLOUDS ROLL BY. An M-G-M (Technicolor) Production based on the life and music of Jerome Kern with Robert Walker as the composer. An all-star cast included Judy Garland, Van Heflin, Lucille Bremer, Dinah Shore, June Allyson, Tony Martin, Kathryn Grayson, Lena Horne, and Frank Sinatra. Featuring Cyd Charisse, Gower Champion, The Wilde Twins, Ray McDonald and Van Johnson. Produced by Arthur Freed. Directed by Richard Whorf. Musical Numbers staged by Robert Alton. Musical Director Lennie Hayton. Orchestrations by Conrad Salinger. Vocal Arrangements by Kay Thompson. Associate Producer Roger Edens.

TILL THE CLOUDS ROLL BY

Words and Music by JEROME KERN
and P.G. WODEHOUSE

She: I'm so sad to think that I have had to drive you from your home so
She: What bad luck, It's com-ing down in buck-ets; Have you an um-brel-la

cool-ly.   *He:* I'd be gain-ing noth-ing by re-main-ing,
hand-y?   *He:* I've a warm coat, wat-er-proof, a storm coat,

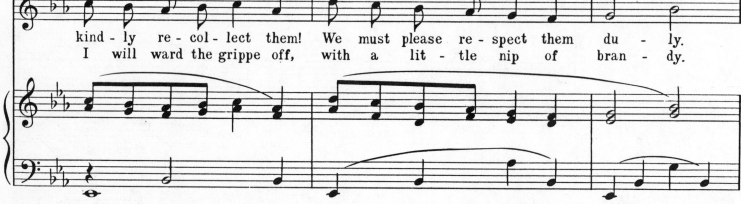

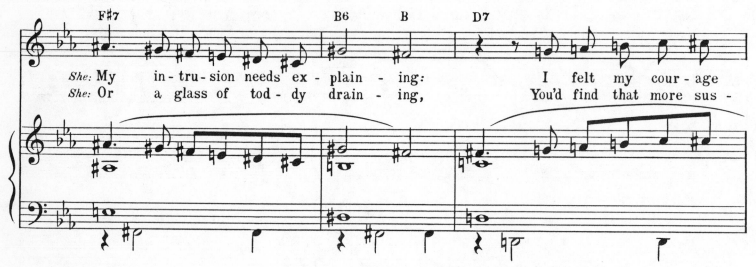

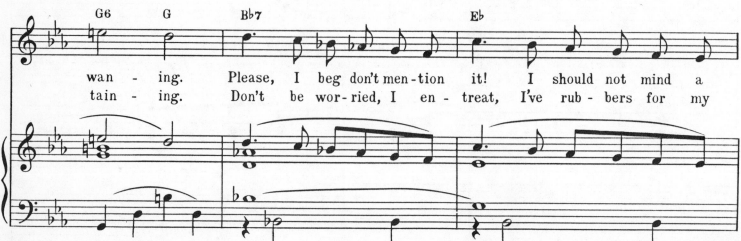

22

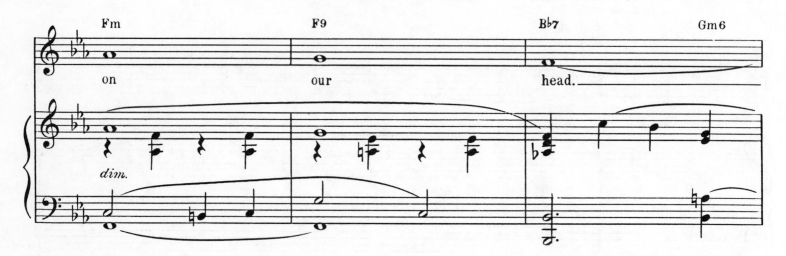

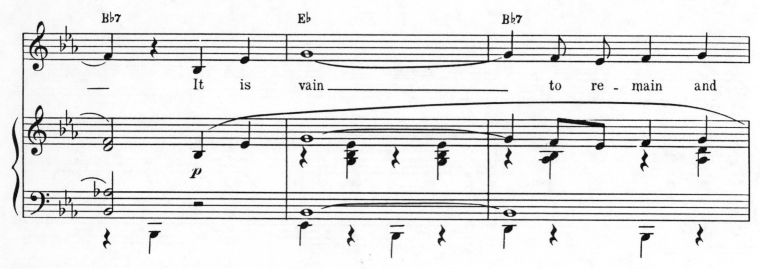

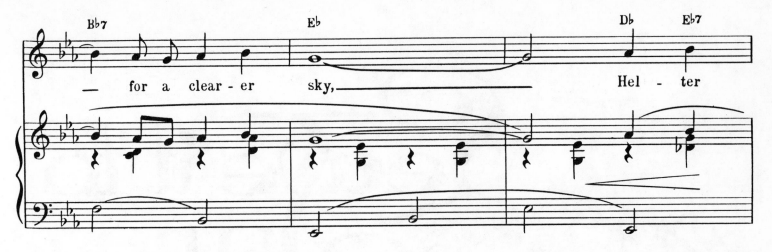

for a clear-er sky,_____ Hel - ter

skel - ter _____ I must fly for shel - ter _____

Till the clouds roll

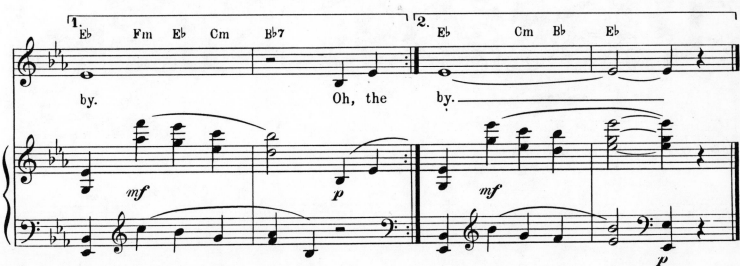

by. Oh, the by._____

Leave it to Jane

LEAVE IT TO JANE: A musical comedy based on George Ade's 1903 comedy "The College Widow" with book and lyrics by Guy Bolton and P. G. Wodehouse. Presented by Morris Gest and Ray Comstock at the Longacre Theatre on August 28, 1917. 167 performances, staged by Edward Royce. The cast included: Edith Hallor, Oscar Shaw, Ann Orr, Arlene Chase, Robert G. Pitkin, Jane Carrol, Georgia O'Ramey, Olin Howland, Rudolf Cutten, Helen Rich and Tess Mayer.

"Gingerbread on the bandstand, banjoes, college blazers, secret fraternity meetings, soft-shoe routines, a touchdown in the last few minutes of the football game and a glorious melodic score by Jerome Kern" is how Emory Lewis described a revival of LEAVE IT TO JANE in his review for Cue Magazine.

Though the plot is simple and lighthearted by today's standards, Alan Dale's review of the 1917 opening for New York American reveals how important LEAVE IT TO JANE was in the transition taking place in musical theatre at the time—a transition, largely spearheaded by Kern, that, when completed, would forever distinguish American musical theatre from shows that were either European in origin or based on European traditions:

"The old timers will soon begin to grieve sorely," wrote Dale, "to tear their hair and gnash their teeth, as they view the new form of rational musical comedy 'getting over' and pushing the old style where it belongs. No more are we asked to laugh at the bottle-nosed comedian as he falls down stairs, no longer is the heroine a lovely princess masquerading as the serving maid, and no more is the scene Ruritania or Monte Carlo. Today is rationally American and the musical show has taken a new lease of life."

Two of the most charming songs from the score are "The Siren's Song" and "Cleopatterer."

THE SIREN'S SONG

Words by P.G. WODEHOUSE
Music by JEROME KERN

singing their sweet de - ceit - ful song. Ma - rin - ers came
sing - ing to - day in mod - ern dress. Just the same they

sail - ing near, Heard that song so soft and clear,
set their snare, Sweet - ly smil - ing false and fair,

An - swered the call that lured them all, And up - on the reef came
Turn a deaf ear when you are near, Or up - on the reef you'll

straight to grief.
come to grief.

Refrain

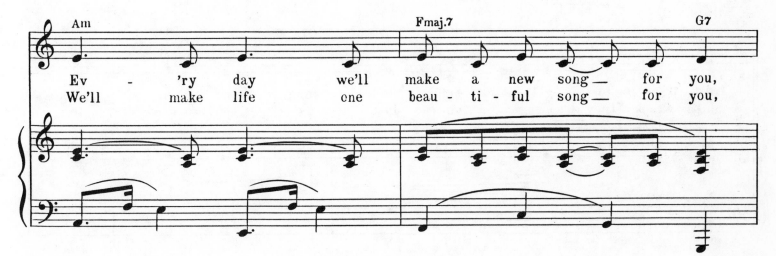

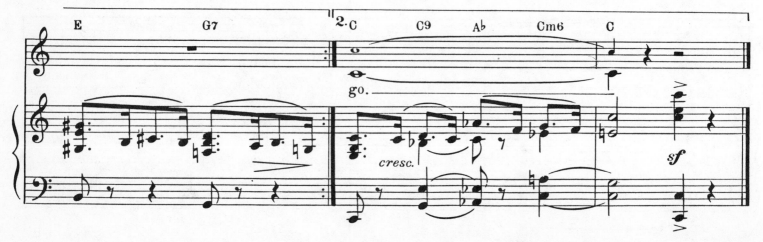

CLEOPATTERER

Words by P.G. WODEHOUSE
Music by JEROME KERN

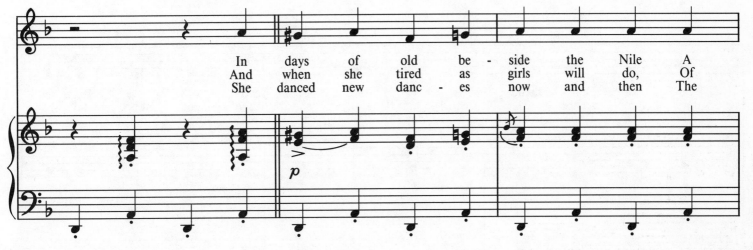

In days of old be-side the Nile A
And when she tired as girls will do, Of
She danced new danc-es now and then The

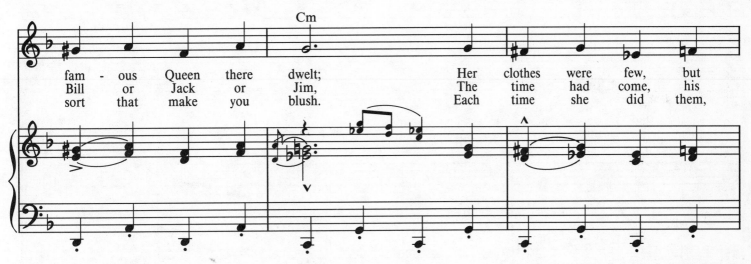

fam-ous Queen there dwelt; Her clothes were few, but
Bill or Jack or Jim, The time had come, his
sort that make you blush. Each time she did them,

full of style; Her fig-ure slim and svelt; On
friends all knew, To say good-bye to him. She
scores of men Got in-jured in the rush. They'd

Burden or Refrain

SALLY. A musical comedy with book by Guy Bolton and P. G. Wodehouse, lyrics by Clifford Grey and B. G. (Buddy) DeSylva, and ballet music by Victor Herbert. Presented by Florenz Ziegfeld at the New Amsterdam Theatre on December 21, 1920. 570 Performances. Staged by Edward Royce. Cast included Marilyn Miller, Walter Catlett and Leon Errol.

With SALLY Kern reverted back to a more traditional kind of musical theatre than The Princess Theatre Shows, a theatre dependent on stars, sets, cast, routines and songs.

As Sally, Marilyn Miller dominated the production. "A Degas figure turned American . . . A Titania of the jazz age," proclaimed the noted critic John Mason Brown. One of the unforgettable moments from the show was her delivery of the touching song "Look For The Silver Lining." The critics also found favor with "Whip-poor-will."

THE MULTI-TALENTED MARILYN MILLER WITH LEON ERROL IN A SCENE FROM "SALLY."

LOOK FOR THE SILVER LINING

Words by BUDDY DeSYLVA
Music by JEROME KERN

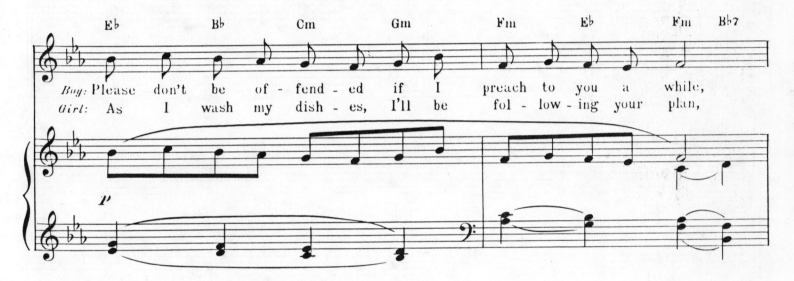

Boy: Please don't be of-fend-ed if I preach to you a while,
Girl: As I wash my dish-es, I'll be fol-low-ing your plan,

Tears are out of place in eyes that were meant to smile.
Till I see the bright-ness in ev-'ry pot and pan.

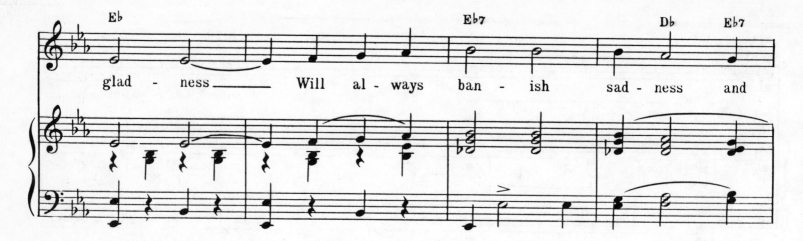

glad - ness _____ Will al - ways ban - ish sad - ness and

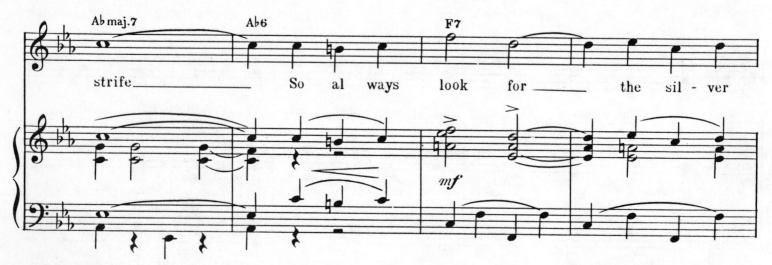

strife _____ So al - ways look for ____ the sil - ver

lin - ing _____ And try to find the sun - ny side of

1. Eb / Bb7 Fm7 Bb7

life.

2. Eb

life. _____

JUDY GARLAND IN HER BRILLIANTLY TOUCHING DELIVERY OF "LOOK FOR THE SILVER LINING" FROM "TILL THE CLOUDS ROLL BY." MISS GARLAND PORTRAYED MARILYN MILLER IN THIS FILM.

WHIP-POOR-WILL

Words by BUD DeSYLVA
Music by JEROME KERN

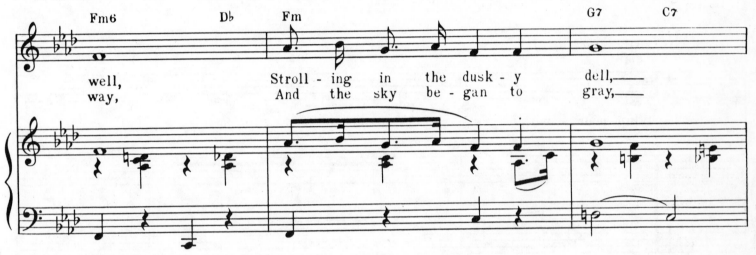

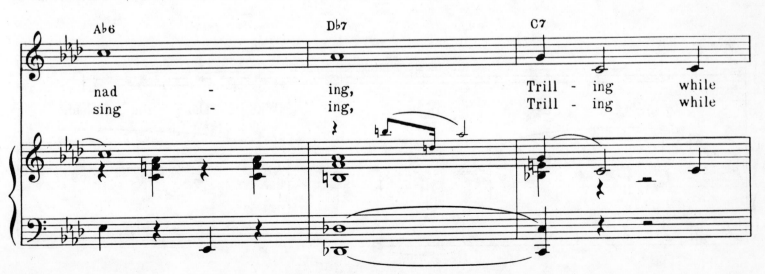

40

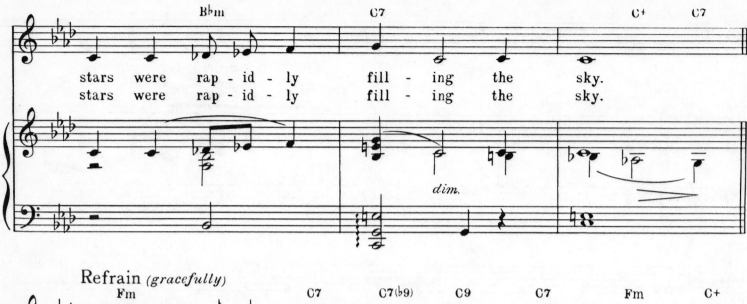

stars were rap - id - ly fill - ing the sky.
stars were rap - id - ly fill - ing the sky.

Refrain *(gracefully)*

Whip-poor-will, I used to love to hear you call to

me. Whip-poor-will,— I know he meant the world and

all to me. When the sun had

41

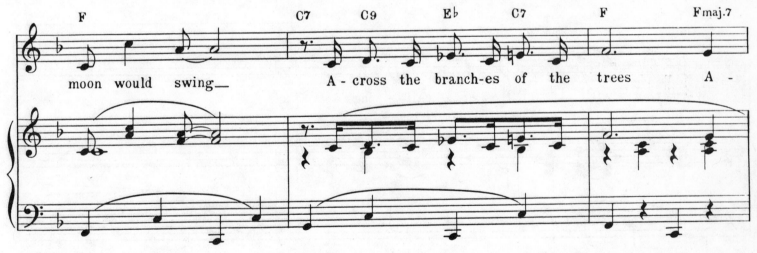

dies   of   love.   Now though you're___ no

long - er   near,___   In my dreams___ I still can hear___

Whip - poor - will___   Ev - er call - ing to me.

me. _____

Good Morning Dearie with book and lyrics by Anne Caldwell. Presented by Charles Dillingham at the Globe Theatre on November 1, 1921. 347 performances. Staged by Edward Royce. Cast included: Louise Groody, Oscar Shaw, William Kent, Ada Lewis, and Harland Dixon. While lavish praise was given to the score as a whole, virtually no critic called specific attention to KA-LU-A, the song that would quickly become the show's most popular and enduring composition.

KA-LU-A

Words by ANNE CALDWELL
Music by JEROME KERN

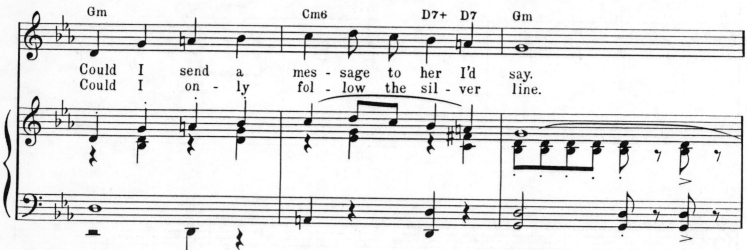

SUNNY. A musical comedy with book and lyrics by Otto Harbach and Oscar Hammerstein II. Presented by Charles Dillingham at the New Amsterdam Theatre on September 22, 1925. 517 Performances. Staged by Hassard Short. Cast included Marilyn Miller, Paul Frawley, Jack Donahue, Mary Hay and Clifton Webb. [Marilyn Miller's musical numbers staged by Fred Astaire.]

Hammerstein recalls an amusing episode:

Before we went into rehearsal Marilyn Miller returned from Europe and met us in Dillingham's office to listen to the story and score we had written so far. We went through the whole plot and described it, and sang whatever numbers we had written up to that point. She seemed to be listening very attentively. When we were all finished there was a pause, and then Marilyn said, "When do I do my tap specialty?"

THE STAR-STUDDED CAST OF "SUNNY," LEFT TO RIGHT: ESTHER HOWARD, JOSEPH CAWTHORN, DOROTHY FRANCIS, CLIFTON WEBB, MARILYN MILLER, PAUL FRAWLEY, MARY HAY AND JACK DONAHUE.

SUNNY

Words by OSCAR HAMMERSTEIN II, OTTO HARBACH
Music by JEROME KERN

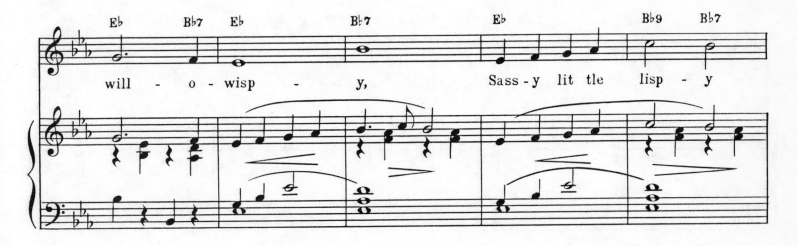

Refrain *(gracefully)*

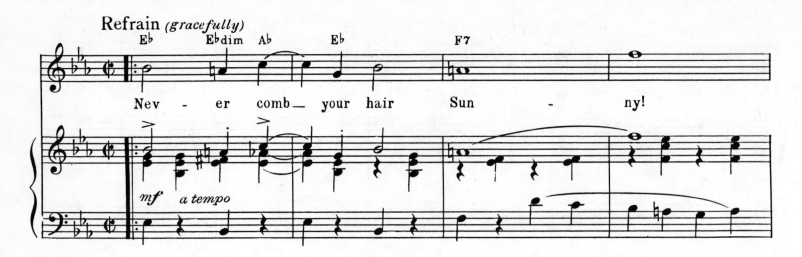

Nev - er comb_ your hair Sun - - ny!

Leave the breez - es there Sun - ny! Let your stock-

-ing fall down, For shock - ing the town is all_

_ that you do. ___ Smil - ing all_ the while

Tom ——————— boy, where'd you get —— your smile

from boy? Lit - tle sun - ny girl,

Be my hon - ey girl, I'm for

you! ——————— you! ——————

WHO?

Words by OTTO HARBACH and OSCAR HAMMERSTEIN II
Music by JEROME KERN

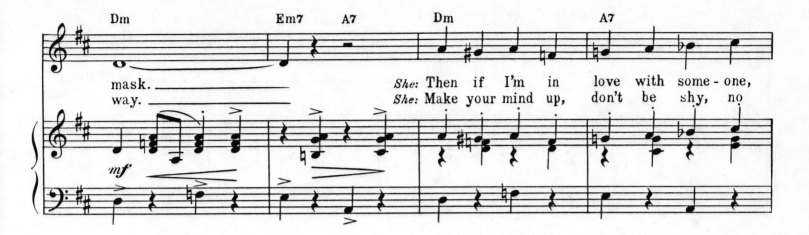

mask. _____
way. _____ *She:* Then if I'm in love with some-one,
She: Make your mind up, don't be shy, no

I must wait un - til there'll come one Boy, who'll know the
game of ee - nie, mee - nie - mi - no Can be played with

an - swer when I ask: _____
la - dies when they say: _____

Refrain *(Smoothly)*

Who _____ stole my heart _____

54

JUDY GARLAND AND THE MALE ENSEMBLE PERFORMING "WHO" IN KERN'S FILMED LIFE STORY "TILL THE CLOUDS ROLL BY."

Hammerstein tells how SHOW BOAT first started:

One day Jerry called me up and said, "How would you like to do a show for Ziegfeld? It's got a million dollar title, Show Boat. I said, "Isn't that Edna Ferber's new book?" Jerry said, "Yes. I haven't finished it yet, but I've already bought it from Ferber. Get a copy and read it right away." "Is Ziegfeld enthusiastic?" I asked. "He doesn't know anything about it yet," said Jerry.

SHOW BOAT. A musical comedy with book and lyrics by Oscar Hammerstein II; adapted from Edna Ferber's novel of the same name. Produced by Florenz Ziegfeld at the Ziegfeld Theatre on December 27, 1927. 572 Performances. Dances and ensembles arranged by Sammy Lee. Scenery by Joseph Urban. Dialogue staged by Mr. Hammerstein. Costumes designed by John Harkrider. Musical director Victor Baravalle. Jubilee singers directed by Will Voudry. Cast included Norma Terris, Howard Marsh, Helen Morgan, Charles Winninger, Edna Mae Oliver, Jules Bledsoe, and Aunt Jemima.

PERHAPS THE MOST DRAMATIC PHOTO OF HELEN MORGAN AS SHE SANG "BILL" IN "SHOW BOAT."

Perhaps the most famous of all the Wodehouse-Kern collaboration will remain the delicately shaped torch song "Bill," which was written in 1918 but was dropped from OH, LADY! LADY! Two years later it was used in the Marilyn Miller show SALLY. Again it was dropped. Finally, in a revised version by Hammerstein, it came to rest in SHOW BOAT. When Helen Morgan sang "Bill" she made it sound as though it had been written expressly for her by Kern and Hammerstein. And, although the lyric credit reads P. G. Wodehouse and Oscar Hammerstein II, the latter made it a point of writing:

I am particularly anxious to point out that the lyric for the song "Bill" was written by P. G. Wodehouse. Although he had always been given credit in the program, it has frequently been assumed that since I wrote all the other lyrics for "Show Boat," I also wrote this one, and I have had praise for it which belonged to another man.

SHOW BOAT

THE MUSICAL THAT REVOLUTIONIZED THE AMERICAN THEATER

CHARLES WINNINGER IN A SCENE FROM ORIGINAL FLORENZ ZIEGFELD PRODUCTION OF "SHOW BOAT."

BILL

Words by P.G. WODEHOUSE and OSCAR HAMMERSTEIN II
Music by JEROME KERN

I used to dream that I would dis-cov-er_ The per-fect lov-er some
He can't play golf, or ten-nis, or po-lo,_ Or sing a so-lo, or

day. I knew I'd re-cog-nize him If ev-er he
row. He is-n't half as hand-some As doz-ens of

SHOW BOAT (First Revival) Produced by Florenz Ziegfeld at the Casino Theatre on May 19, 1932. 180 Performances. Essentially the same cast as the original production, with the major exceptions of the substitution of Paul Robeson and Dennis King. Including Eva Puck, Sammy White, William Kent, Helen Morgan, and Norma Terris.

SHOW BOAT. (Film—1936) A second screen version with screenplay by Mr. Hammerstein. Produced by Carl Laemmle, Jr. for Universal Pictures. Directed by James Whale. Released on May 14, 1936. Cast included Irene Dunne, Allan Jones, Charles Winninger, Paul Robeson, Helen Morgan, Helen Westley, Donald Cook, Queenie Smith, Sammy White, Hattie McDaniel and Patricia Barry.

MIRIAM HOPKINS, IRENE DUNNE, HELEN MORGAN, DONALD COOK AND CHARLES WINNINGER FROM THE 1936 SCREEN PRODUCTION OF "SHOW BOAT."

CAN'T HELP LOVIN' DAT MAN

Words by OSCAR HAMMERSTEIN II
Music by JEROME KERN

De an - gels done plan. ____

De chimb-ley's smok-in', De roof is leak-in' in, ____ But he don't ____

____ seem to care, He can be hap-py Wid jus' a sip of

gin. ____ I ev - en loves him when ____

— his kiss - es got gin. _____

Refrain *(slowly)*

Fish got to swim and birds got to fly,— I got to love_ one

man till I die,— Can't help lov - in' dat man_ of

mine. _____ Tell me he's la - zy,

tell me he's slow,   Tell me I'm cra - zy, may-be, I know,—

Can't help   lov - in' dat man__ of   mine._____

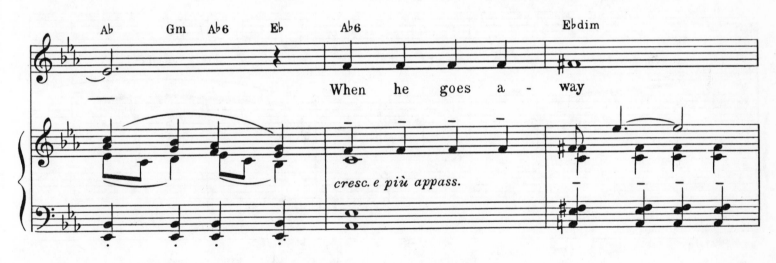

When he goes a - way

Dat's a rain - y   day,   And when he comes

SHOW BOAT. (Revival—1946) A third New York production presented by Mr. Kern and Mr. Hammerstein. Staged by Hassard Short. Directed by Oscar Hammerstein II. Costumes by Lucinda Ballard. Sets Designed by Howard Bay. Musical Director, Edwin MacArthur, Dances by Helen Tamaris. At the Ziegfeld Theatre on January 5, 1946. 418 Performances. Cast included Buddy Ebsen, Carol Bruce, Jan Clayton, Max Showalter, Pearl Primus, Ethel Owen and Charles Fredericks.

SHOW BOAT. (Revival—1948) A fourth New York production presented by Richard Rodgers and Oscar Hammerstein II at The New York City Center on September 7, 1948 with a cast including Carol Bruce, Norwood Smith, Ruth Gates and Billy House.

SHOW BOAT. (Film—1951) A third screen version presented by Metro-Goldwyn-Mayer in Technicolor and released on July 19, 1951. Produced by Arthur Freed. Directed by George Sidney. Musical Numbers Staged by Robert Alton. Associate Producer Roger Edens. Musical Direction by Adolph Deutsch. Orchestrations by Conrad Salinger. Vocal Arrangements by Robert Tucker. Costumes designed Walter Plunkett. Director of Photography Charles Rosher. Art Direction by Jack Martin Smith. Cast included Kathryn Grayson, Ava Gardner, Howard Keel, Joe E. Brown, Marge and Gower Champion, Robert Sterling, Agnes Moorehead, Adele Jergens, Leif Erickson and William Warfield.

From the MGM Release "Show Boat" © 1951 Loew's Incorporated

MGM'S ALL-STAR "SHOW BOAT" CAST (LEFT TO RIGHT) KATHRYN GRAYSON, HOWARD KEEL, AVA GARDNER, JOE E. BROWN, AGNES MOOREHEAD AND ROBERT STERLING.

MAKE BELIEVE

Words by OSCAR HAMMERSTEIN II
Music by JEROME KERN

tend - ing; ____ Could - n't you? Could - n't I? Could - n't

____ make be - lieve our lips ____ are blend - ing ____ In a

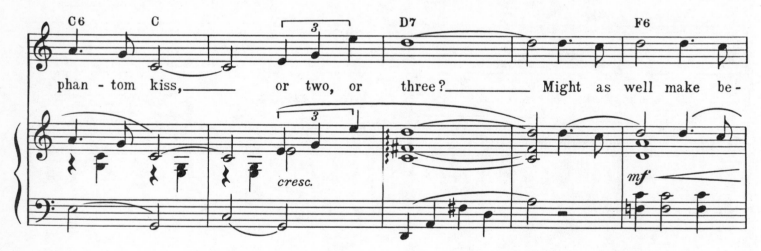

phan - tom kiss, ____ or two, or three? ____ Might as well make be -

lieve I love you, ____ For, To tell the truth, ____ I

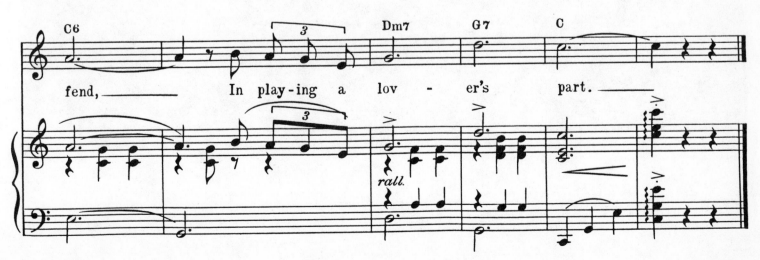

In her autobiography, A PECULIAR TREASURE, Edna Ferber describes her emotional response when she first heard this song:

As the writing of the musical play proceeded I heard bits and pieces of the score . . . I had heard "Can't Help Lovin' Dat Man" with its love-bemused lyric . . . I had melted under the bewitching strains of "Make Believe" and of "Why Do I Love You?" . . . And then Jerome Kern appeared at my apartment late one afternoon with a strange look of quiet exultation in his eyes. He sat down at the piano. He didn't play the piano particularly well and his singing voice, though true, was negligible. He played and sang "Ol' Man River." The music mounted, mounted, and I give you my word my hair stood on end, the tears came to my eyes, I breathed like a heroine in a melodrama. This was great music. This was music that would outlast Jerome Kern's day and mine. I never have heard it since without that emotional surge.

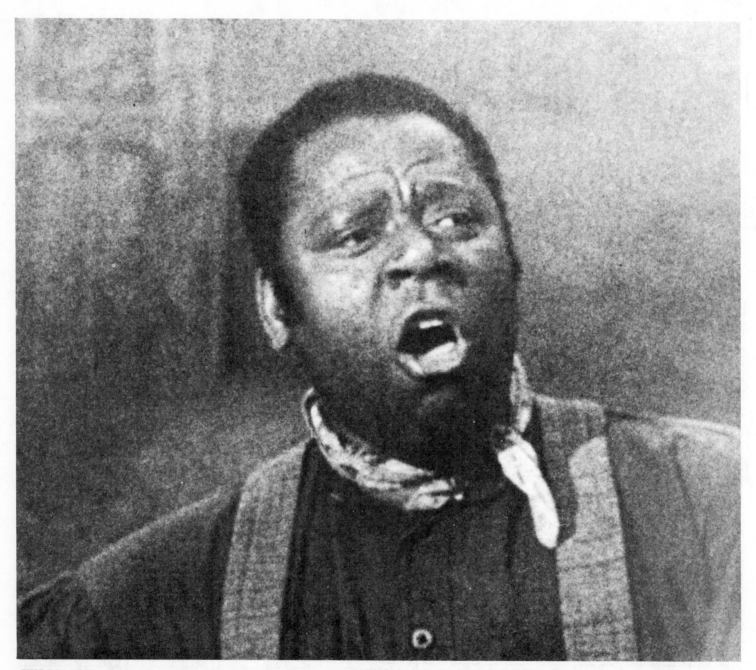

WILLIAM WARFIELD GIVES HIS MAGNIFICENT RENDITION OF "OL' MAN RIVER" IN THE MGM/ARTHUR FREED 1951 FILM VERSION OF "SHOW BOAT."

OL' MAN RIVER

Words by OSCAR HAMMERSTEIN II
Music by JEROME KERN

Dat's de ol' stream dat I long to cross.

Refrain *(very slowly, with deep expression)*

Ol' man riv-er, dat ol' man riv-er, He must know sump-in', but

don't say noth-in', He jus' keeps roll-in', He keeps on roll-in' a-

long. He don't plant 'ta-ters, he

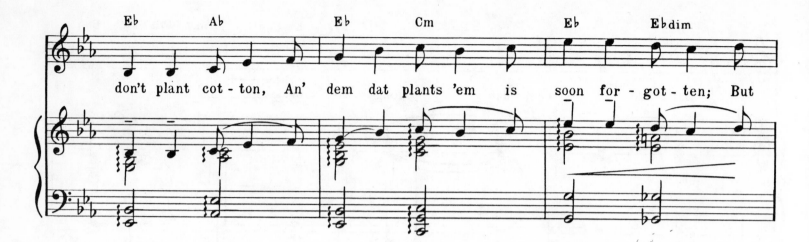

don't plant cot - ton, An' dem dat plants 'em is soon for - got - ten; But

ol' man riv - er, he jus' keeps roll - in' a - long.

You an' me, we sweat an' strain,

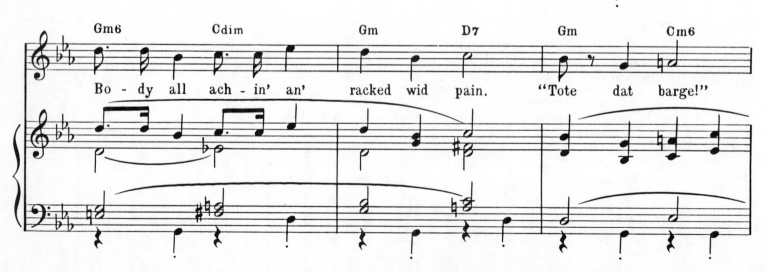

Bo - dy all ach - in' an' racked wid pain. "Tote dat barge!"

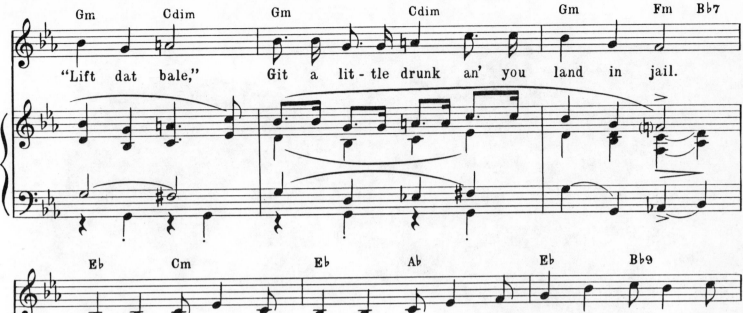

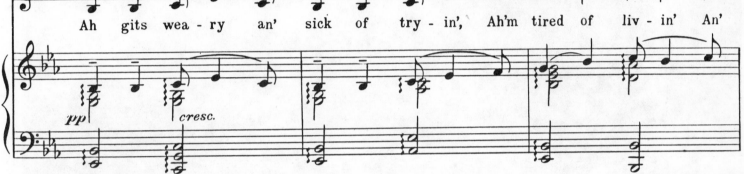

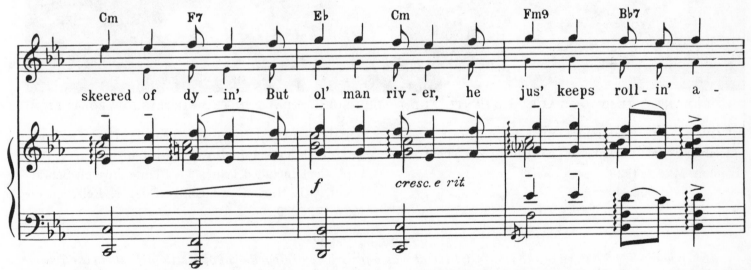

THE ROMANTIC TEAM OF LAURA LaPLANTE AND JOSEPH SCHILDKRAUT IN THE FIRST "SHOW BOAT" FILM.

SHOW BOAT. (Original London Production) Produced by Felix Edwardes at the Drury Lane Theatre, London, May 3, 1928.

SHOW BOAT. (Film) Produced by Carl Laemmle Jr. for Universal Pictures. Directed by Harry Pollard. Cast included Laura La Plante, Joseph Schildkraut, Otis Harlan and Emily Fitzroy. Released on May 17, 1929.

"Why Do I Love You?"

Kern had a blind hatred of the word CUPID; it was a favorite word-symbol of operetta lyricists in the Twenties and therefore represented to Kern everything that was corny and old-fashioned in the Viennese school of musical theater. One day while SHOW BOAT was going through its out-of-town tryout Kern gave Hammerstein a tune to set words to. He had worked on it, as he always did, with infinite patience and unbridled enthusiasm and breathlessly awaited the results of Hammerstein's romp with the Muse. Hammerstein, alone in his hotel room, worked out a lyric titled "Why Do I Love You?", but out of some perverse whimsicality also dashed off another lyric on the opposite side of the paper. He handed the latter side to Kern, who snatched at it, propped it on the piano, and started to sing it in his usual wild, impassioned screech. Here is how it began:

CUPID KNOWS THE WAY
by Oscar Hammerstein II

CUPID KNOWS THE WAY; HE'S A NAKED BOY. WHO CAN MAKE YOU SWAY TO LOVE'S OWN JOY. WHEN HE SHOOTS HIS LITTLE ARROW, HE CAN THRILL YOU TO THE MARROW . . .

After the initial shock, Kern laughed as heartily as Hammerstein. He also laughed a great deal longer, for he subsequently framed the lyric carefully and displayed it prominently in his home for all visitors to see, the author's name clearly visible. The visitors were not told, however, that it had been written as a joke.

WHY DO I LOVE YOU?

Words by OSCAR HAMMERSTEIN II
Music by JEROME KERN

I'm in _____ the sev-enth heav - en _____ (There's more than

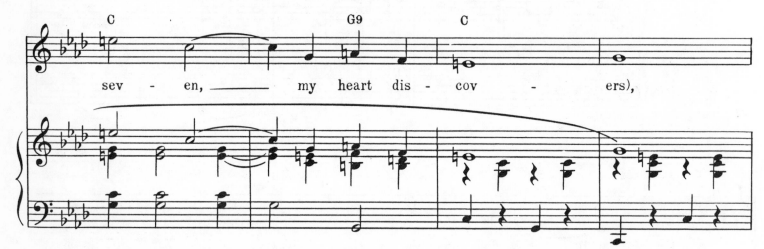

sev - en, _____ my heart dis - cov - ers),

In this sweet, im - prob - a - ble and un - real world,

Find - ing you has giv-en me my i - deal world.

cresc.

83

SHOW BOAT. (Revival—1954) A fifth New York production produced by the New York City Opera Company and Light Opera Company. Staged by William Hammerstein. New York City Center on April 8, 1954 (Opera); May 5, 1954 (Light Opera). Opera cast included: Laurel Hurley, Robert Rounseville, Helena Bliss, Marjorie Gateson and Jack Albertson. Light Opera cast included: Burl Ives, Donn Driver, Lawrence Winters and Helen Phillips.

SHOW BOAT. (London Revival—1971) A second London production produced by Harold Fielding at London's Adelphi Theatre on July 29, 1971. Directed and Choreographed by Wendy Toye. Musical Direction and Dance Music Arrangements by Ray Cook. 499 Performances. Cast included Andre Jobin, Cleo Laine, Thomas Carey, Kenneth Nelson and Derek Royle.

LENA HORNE, LEFT, PORTRAYING JULIE, WILLIAM HALLIGAN AS CAPTAIN ANDY, VIRGINIA O'BRIEN AS ELLIE AND BRUCE COWLING AS STEVE IN THE "SHOW BOAT" SCENE FROM THE 1946 MUSICAL "TILL THE CLOUDS ROLL BY."

YOU ARE LOVE

Words by OSCAR HAMMERSTEIN II
Music by JEROME KERN

was gay.———— But I knew the joke was aim-less,

Time went on, I liked the game less, for you see,————

— Some-where lurked a spark di-vine and I kept won-d'ring

wheth-er mine would come to me.————

Poco agitato

Then___ my for - tune turned and I found you;

Here___ you are with my arms a - round you.

You___ will nev - er know what you've meant___ to me.

You're___ the prize that heav - en has sent___ to me.

Here's — a bright and beau-ti-ful world — all new Wrapped

Tempo di Valse

up — in you.

Refrain *(with expression)*

You — are love, here in my arms

Where you be-long, And here you will stay. I'll not let you a-

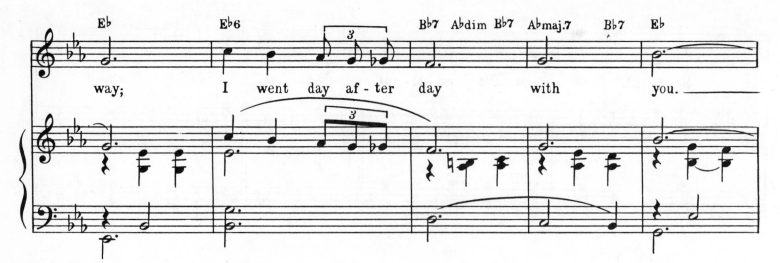

way; I went day af-ter day with you.

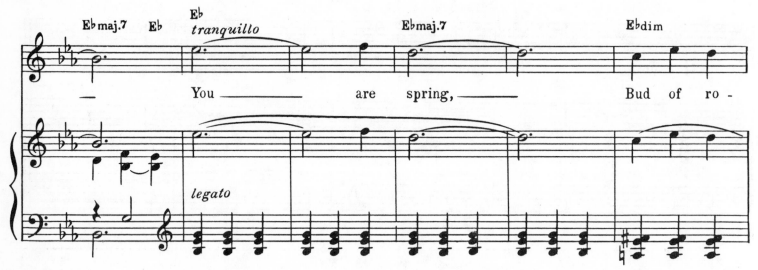

You are spring, Bud of ro-

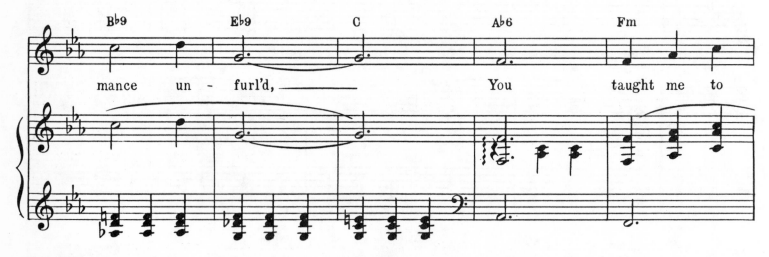

mance un-furl'd, You taught me to

see One truth for-ev-er true.

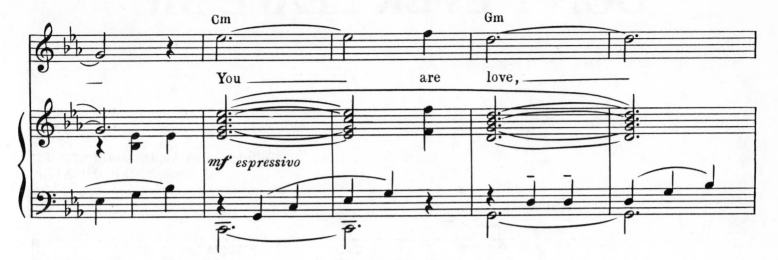

DON'T EVER LEAVE ME

Words by OSCAR HAMMERSTEIN II
Music by JEROME KERN

Moderato

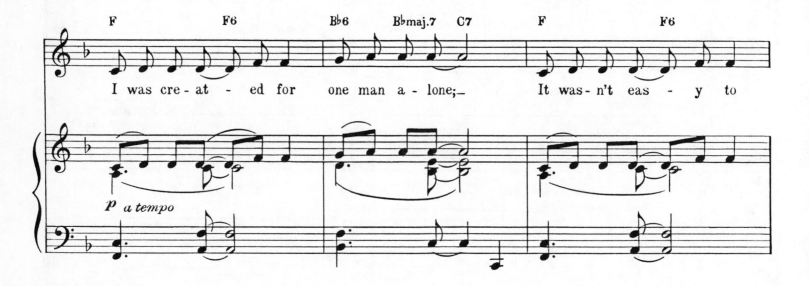

I was cre-at-ed for one man a-lone;___ It was-n't eas-y to

find. Now that I found___ him, I won-der just how___

I could have lived— right up to now;— Now I am some - thing com-

plet - ed by you,— I am no one,— just part of two.—

Refrain *(not fast)*

Don't ev - er leave— me, now that you're here!— Here is where you— be -

long. Ev - 'ry - thing seems so right when you're near,—

94

Over the July 4th weekend in 1929 the Oscar Hammersteins were guests aboard the Kerns' yacht, *the Show Boat,* anchored off New London, Connecticut. Kern played the melody for this song and Hammerstein, quite touched by its beauty, worked out a lyric titled "Don't Ever Leave Me" which he dedicated to his wife, Dorothy, whom he had married two months earlier.

HUGH HERBERT, LOUIS CALHERN, IRENE DUNNE, DONALD WOODS, JOSEPH CAWTHORN AND NED SPARKS IN THE 1935 MOTION PICTURE VERSION OF "SWEET ADELINE."

96

SWEET ADELINE. A musical romance with book and lyrics by Oscar Hammerstein II. Presented by Arthur Hammerstein at the Hammerstein Theatre on September 2, 1929. 234 Performances. Book staged by Reginald Hammerstein. Dances and ensembles staged by Danny Dare. It starred Helen Morgan and featured Charles Butterworth, Irene Franklin and Robert Chisholm.

Helen Morgan, although not actually starred in *Show Boat,* walked away with all the singing and acting honors, and was rewarded by having the next Kern and Hammerstein musical, SWEET ADELINE, written especially for her.

The particular area of popular art that Helen Morgan staked out for herself was a severely limited

one, but surely no one has ever done more within a chosen area. Like Ruth Etting and Libby Holman, she was a symbol of a particular type of femininity: mournful, gamely vanquished, singing in a brave little voice about the sadder aspects of love. The well-remembered image of Helen Morgan sitting atop a piano and spinning out her songs with a rare artistry has never faded, and in retrospect it seems odd that her voice was the high, sweet instrument it was, rather than the deeper, more sultry sound that her materials appeared to demand. Nevertheless, she epitomized in many respects the end of an era, those disturbing years of the late Twenties and early Thirties, and left behind her a haunting and tantalizing memory.

HELEN MORGAN AND CHARLES BUTTERWORTH IN A SCENE FROM "SWEET ADELINE" IN WHICH SHE INTRODUCED THE MOVING "WHY WAS I BORN?"

WHY WAS I BORN

Words by OSCAR HAMMERSTEIN II
Music by JEROME KERN

Andante con moto

Spend-ing these lone-some eve _ nings With noth-ing to do but to live in dreams that I

make up,___ All by my-self;___

Dream-ing that you're be - side me, I pic - ture the pret-ti - est sto - ries on - ly to

wake up,_____ All by my - self._____

What is the good of me, by my - self?_____ *L.H.*

poco rit

Refrain

Why was I born?_____ Why am I

p a tempo

con pedale

liv - ing?_____ What do I get?_____ What am I

giv - ing? Why do I want a thing I dare - n't hope for?_____

_____ What can I hope for?_____ I wish I knew._____

_____ Why do I try_____ To draw you

near me?_____ Why do I cry?_____ You nev - er

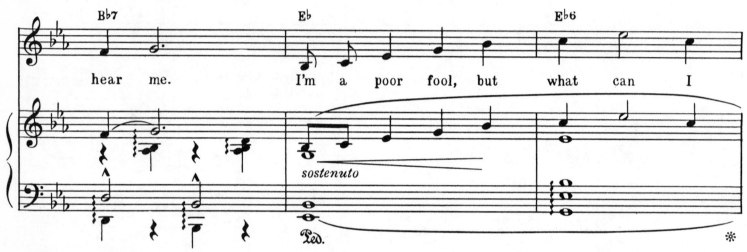

hear me. I'm a poor fool, but what can I

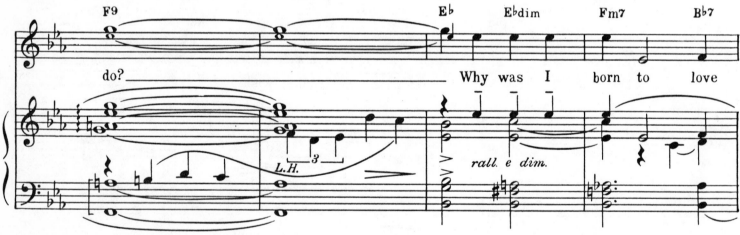

do?_____ Why was I born to love

you? you?

SHE DIDN'T SAY "YES"

Words and Music by
JEROME KERN

She did-n't say "Yes," She did-n't say "No," She did-n't say "stay," She
She did-n't say "Yes," She did-n't say "No," She want-ed to stay, But

did-n't say "go," She on-ly knew that he had spied her there____
knew she should go, She was-n't so sure that he'd be good____

C *(Tacet)*   **D9**   **G7**   **A**   **A6**

— And then she knew he sat be - side her there. At first there was heard Not
— She was - n't ev - en sure that she'd be good. She want - ed to rest All

Bm7   **E7(A) E7**   **C**   **C6**   **Dm7**   **G7(C) G7**

one lit - tle word, Then coy - ly she took One sly lit - tle look And
cud - dled and pressed A pal - pa - ble part Of some - bod - y's heart. She

C   **C+**   **Fmaj.7 F6 Cdim**   **C**   *(Tacet)*

some - thing a - woke and smiled in - side, _____ Her heart be - gan beat - ing
loved to be "en rap - port" with him, _____ But not be - hind a bolt - ed

Am7   **D9**   **C**   **D7**

wild in - side. So what did she do? I leave it to you, She
door with him. And what did she do? I leave it to you, She

C (Tacet) ... **D9 G7** ... **A** ... **A6**

For well she knew 'twas on-ly safe out-side. In there it was warm, Out
And yet she knew there'd be a reck-on-ing. She want-ed to climb, But

Bm7 **E7(A) E7** ... **C** **C6** ... **Dm7** **G7(C) G7** ... **C** ... **C+**

there it was cold The sleet and the storm Said "Bet-ter be bold!" She mur-mured: "I'm not a-
dread-ed to fall So bid-ed her time And clung to the wall, She want-ed to act ad

Fmaj.7 F6 Cdim ... **C** (Tacet) ... **Am7** **D9**

fraid of ice_____ I on-ly wish that I was made of ice." So
li-bi-tum,_____ But feared to lose her e-qui-lib-ri-um. So

C ... **D7** ... **G7** ... **C**

what did she do? I leave it to you, She did just what you'd do too._____
what did she do? I leave it to you, She did just what you'd do too._____

D. S.

THE CAT AND THE FIDDLE. A musical comedy with book and lyrics by Otto Harbach. Presented by Max Gordon and the Globe Theatre on October 15, 1931. 395 Performances. Staged by José Ruben. Cast included Odette Myrtil, George Meader, Georges Metaxa and Bettina Hall.

ANOTHER KERN LOVE DUO: JEANETTE McDONALD AND RAMON NAVARRO IN THE FILM VERSION OF "THE CAT AND THE FIDDLE," WHICH INCLUDED THE PRECEDING SONG, "SHE DIDN'T SAY YES" AND "THE NIGHT WAS MADE FOR LOVE."

THE NIGHT
WAS MADE FOR LOVE

Words by OTTO HARBACH
Music by JEROME KERN

sweet del - i - cate charms,_____ But night time sighs for ___

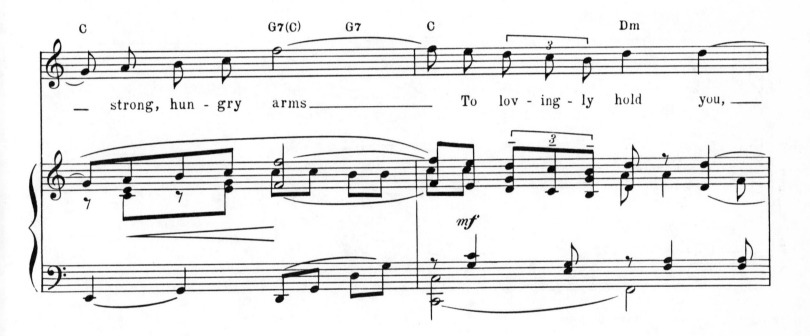

___ strong, hun - gry arms_____ To lov - ing - ly hold you, ___

___ while two lips on fire:_____ Have ar - dent - ly told you ___

MUSIC IN THE AIR. A musical comedy with book and lyrics by Oscar Hammerstein II. Presented by Peggy Fears and A. C. Blumenthall at the Alvin Theatre on November 8, 1932. 342 Performances. Staged by Mr. Hammerstein and Mr. Kern. Cast included Walter Slezak, Katherine Carrington, Tullio Carminati and Al Shean.

"At last the musical drama has been emancipated," proclaimed Brooks Atkinson in his *New York Times* review on the day following the opening of this show. "Jerome Kern and Oscar Hammerstein 2nd have succeeded in telling a romantic story without recourse to the super-anuated formula . . . What *The Cat and the Fiddle* gallantly began last season Messrs. Kern and Hammerstein have now completed: a fable that flows naturally out of a full-brimming score."

THE HERO AND HEROINE OF "MUSIC IN THE AIR" WALTER SLEZAK AND KATHERINE CARRINGTON AS THEY SANG "I'VE TOLD EV'RY LITTLE STAR" AND "THE SONG IS YOU."

"I've Told Ev'ry Little Star"

"Jerry got the melodic theme from a bird. He swears it!" Hammerstein wrote his colleague Sigmund Romberg. "He heard a finch outside his window singing the first line and he built a refrain on it." Kern and Hammerstein were further indebted to the finch because they opened MUSIC IN THE AIR with this very episode: a composer getting inspiration from a bird song. "Incidentally," Hammerstein added, " 'Ev'ry Little Star' proved to be a stubborn tune and for a whole summer resisted my efforts to set words to it. There were times during those hot August days when I wished the finch had kept his big mouth shut!"

I'VE TOLD EV'RY LITTLE STAR

Words by OSCAR HAMMERSTEIN II
Music by JEROME KERN

112

sigh _____ Oh, dear.

poco deliberato e marcato

Refrain *(gracefully)*

I've told ev-'ry lit-tle star, Just how sweet I

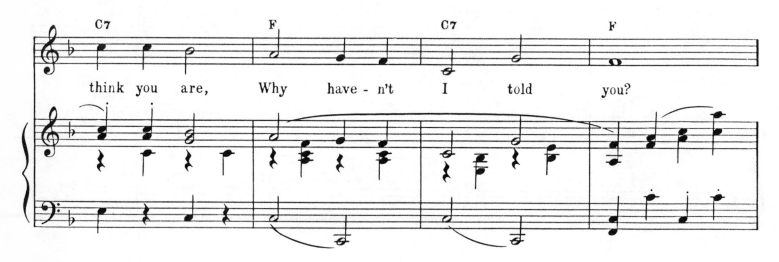

think you are, Why have-n't I told you?

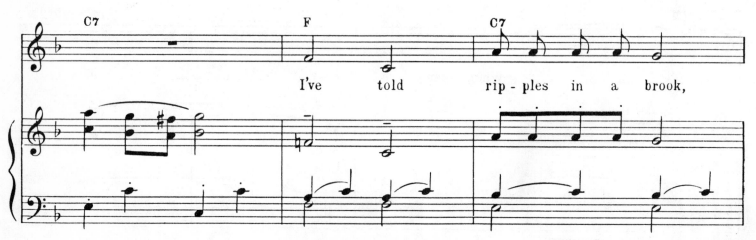

I've told rip-ples in a brook,

Made my heart an o-pen book, Why have-n't I told

you?_____ Friends ask me: Am

I in love? I al-ways an-swer "Yes,"

Might as well con-fess, If I don't, they guess.

114

Maybe you may know it too, Oh, my dar-ling,

if you do, Why have-n't you told me?

THE SONG IS YOU

Words by OSCAR HAMMERSTEIN II
Music by JEROME KERN

start, _____ Then melt a - way. I hear mu-sic when I touch your

hand, _____ A beau - ti - ful mel - o - dy from some en - chant - ed

land, _____ Down deep in my heart, _____ I hear it

say, _____ Is this the day? _____

let you know the song my heart would sing, _____ That beau - ti - ful

rhap - so - dy of love and youth and spring, _____ The mu - sic is

sweet, _____ The words are true, _____ The song is

you. _____

SMOKE GETS IN YOUR EYES

Words by OTTO HARBACH
Music by JEROME KERN

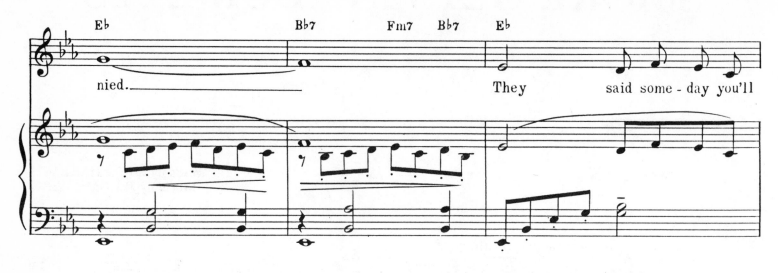

nied._____ They said some - day you'll

find, All who love are blind,_____ When your heart's on

fire, You must re - al - ize Smoke gets in your eyes._____

Un poco piu mosso

So I chaffed them and I gay - ly laughed_ to think they could doubt my

ROBERTA

THE BROADWAY SHOW THAT
INTRODUCED THREE GREAT
SONGS
"THE TOUCH OF YOUR HAND",
"YESTERDAYS"
AND
"SMOKE GETS IN YOUR EYES"

ROBERTA. A musical comedy with book and lyrics by Otto Harbach. Based on Alice Duer Miller's novel *Gowns by Roberta*. "I'll Be Hot to Handle" lyrics by Bernard Dougall. Presented by Max Gordon at the New Amsterdam Theatre on November 18, 1933. 295 Performances. Staged by Hassard Short. Cast included Tamara, Ray Middleton, Bob Hope, Fay Templeton, George Murphy, Sydney Greenstreet and Fred MacMurray.

This was the show that skyrocketed Bob Hope to fame. It was also, by coincidence, the last stage appearance of Fay Templeton, a great Broadway star for over three decades.

"Smoke Gets In Your Eyes"

It took two false starts before this song saw the great light of day. Kern originally had composed it as the signature theme for a radio series but the project collapsed before it went on the air. Again as an instrumental, it was used for a tap routine in SHOW BOAT in front of the show curtain while the scenery was being changed. During the out-of-town tryouts the scene change was eliminated and so was the number. Otto Harbach stumbled across the manuscripts while at work on ROBERTA. "Why not change the tempo," he asked Kern, "if these short notes might be made long notes might it not make an attractive ballad?" Kern agreed, and the end result was "Smoke Gets In Your Eyes."

(The song, thought by most people to be Kern's most well known work, starts on page 98)

FOUR OF THE PRINCIPALS, LEFT TO RIGHT, GEORGE MURPHY, RAY MIDDLETON, TAMARA, AND BOB HOPE.

THE TOUCH OF YOUR HAND

Words by OTTO HARBACH
Music by JEROME KERN

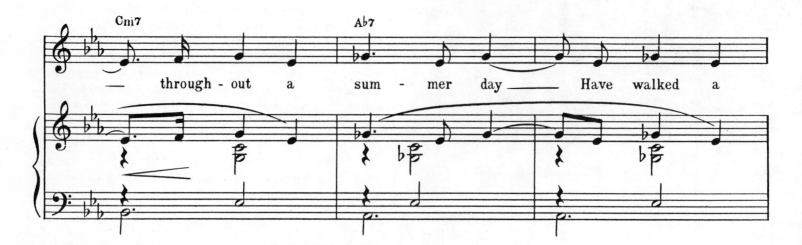

125

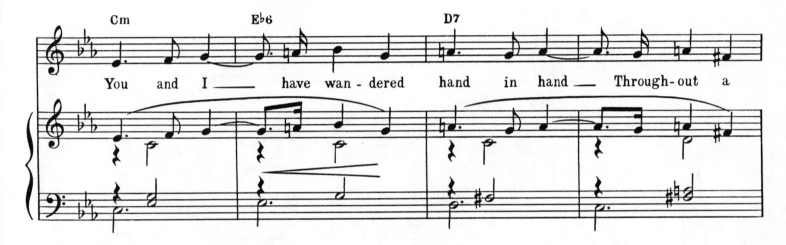

Where the sky and blue hor - i - zon blend.

Yet we've both walked our one last mile,

It's good - bye for a while.

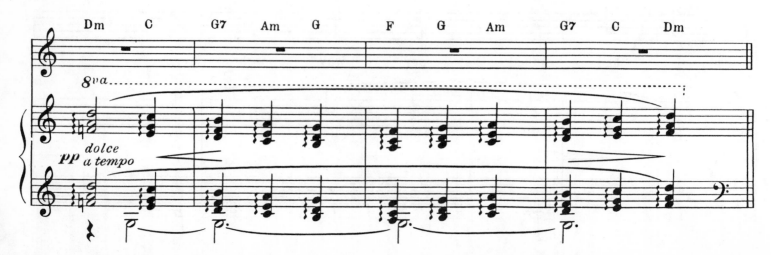

Allegretto con anima

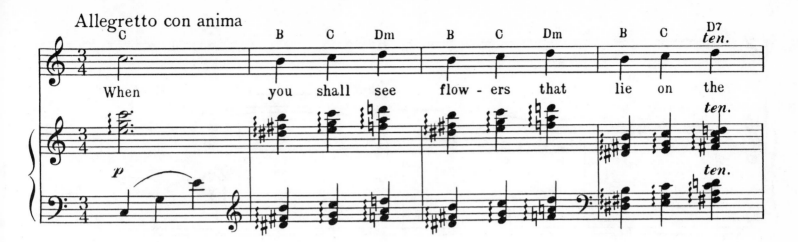

When you shall see flow-ers that lie on the

plain, Ly - ing there sigh - ing for one touch of

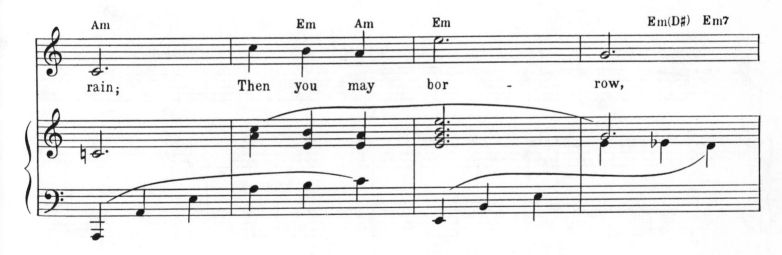

rain; Then you may bor - row,

Some glimpse of my sor - row,

And you'll un - der - stand _____ How I

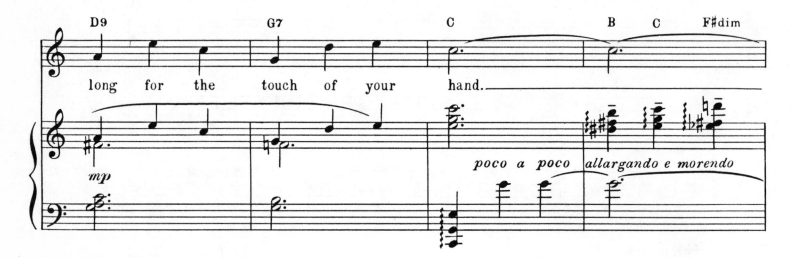

long for the touch of your hand. _____

YESTERDAYS

Words by OTTO HARBACH
Music by JEROME KERN

Andantino quasi allegretto

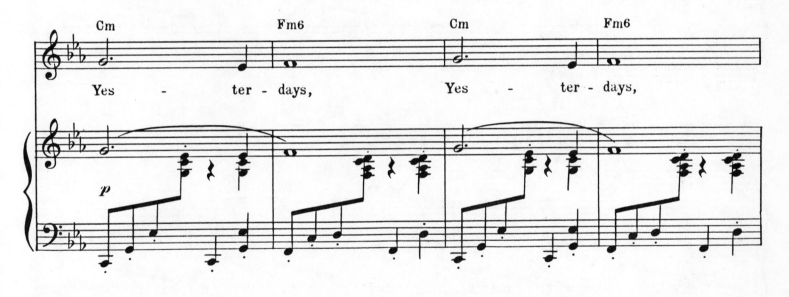

Old - en days, Gold - en days,

Days of mad ro - mance and love, Then gay

youth was mine, Truth was mine,

Joy - ous, free and flam - ing life for - sooth was mine.

Sad am I, Glad am I,

For to-day I'm dream-ing of yes - ter -

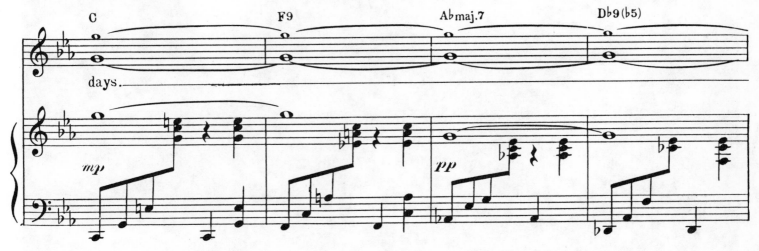

days.

VERY WARM FOR MAY. A Musical comedy with book and lyrics by Oscar Hammerstein II. Presented by Max Gordon at the Alvin Theatre on November 17, 1939. 59 Performances. Staged by Vincente Minnelli. Dances staged by Albertina Rasch and Harry Losee. Book directed by Mr. Hammerstein. Cast included Grace McDonald, Jack Whiting, Hiram Sherman and Donald Brian.

TONY MARTIN, WHO HAD ONE OF HIS MOST OUTSTANDING SUCCESSES WITH "ALL THE THINGS YOU ARE" AND THE COMPOSER IN 1939.

"All The Things You Are" was one of the most surprising hits Kern and Hammerstein had. They never thought the public would take to it because the middle of the refrain contains three changes of key.

ALL THE THINGS YOU ARE

Words by OSCAR HAMMERSTEIN II
Music by JEROME KERN

Time and a-gain I've longed for ad-ven-ture, Some-thing to make my

heart beat the fast-er. What did I long for? I nev-er real-ly

knew. Find-ing your love I've found my ad-ven-ture,

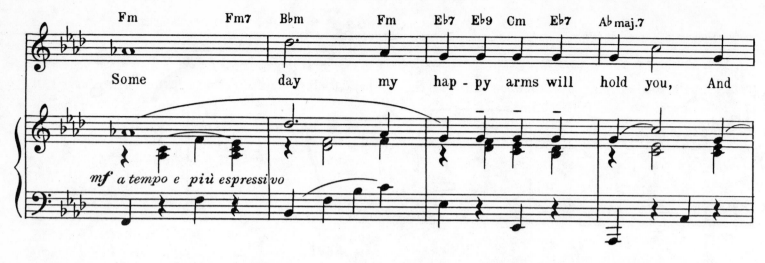

ROBERTA. An RKO Picture released in March, 1935. Starred Irene Dunne, Fred Astaire and Ginger Rogers; featured Randolph Scott and Helen Westley. Lyrics by Otto Harbach, Bernard Dougall, Oscar Hammerstein II, Dorothy Fields and Jimmy McHugh. Produced by Pandro S. Berman. Directed by William A. Seiter.

ROBERTA was the start of Jerome Kern in Hollywood. (His score for the 1931 film THE MAN IN THE SKY cannot be counted because Warner Brothers cut all the songs and released it as MEN OF THE SKY, a straight picture.) This film version of his recent stage success also served to introduce him to a woman who became one of his most important collaborators: Dorothy Fields.

Miss Fields recounted this to me: "It's very curious how I first started working with Jerry. Of course, he knew my father and my brothers [her father was the famous Broadway Actor-Producer, Lew Fields, who was also part of that famous comedy team, Weber and Fields. Her brothers were Herbert and Joseph, both Broadway playwrights]. I was working at RKO and Pan Berman, who was producing ROBERTA, asked me if I'd take a couple of days and work on it. He said, 'we have a seriously uneven melody of Jerome Kern's that he's given us to add to the score; it needs a lyric . . .' So I wrote 'Lovely To Look At,' which absolutely astounded Berman. And he had the nerve to tell Bill Seiter, the director, to go ahead and shoot it — the whole sequence — and Jerry hadn't even okayed the lyric! Well, I don't have to tell you Jerry loved it and from then on — he asked for me."

GINGER ROGERS AND FRED ASTAIRE IN THEIR FIRST KERN MUSICAL TOGETHER.

"I Won't Dance" first appeared in the Kern-Hammerstein London musical THREE SISTERS early in 1934. Later that same year, with the Hammerstein title but an almost totally new lyric by Dorothy Fields and Jimmy McHugh, it served as a brilliant song and dance number for Fred Astaire in the film version of Roberta.

KERN IN HOLLYWOOD

I WON'T DANCE

Words by OSCAR HAMMERSTEIN II & OTTO HARBACH
Screen Version by DOROTHY FIELDS & JIMMY McHUGH
Music by JEROME KERN

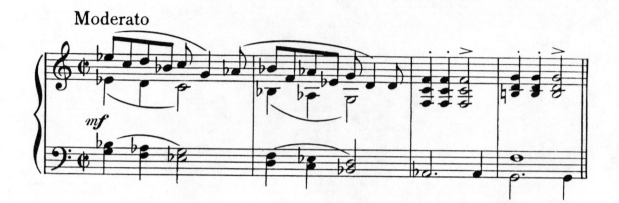

Think of what you're los-ing By con-stant-ly re-fus-ing to

dance with me._____ You'd be the i-dol of France with me!_____

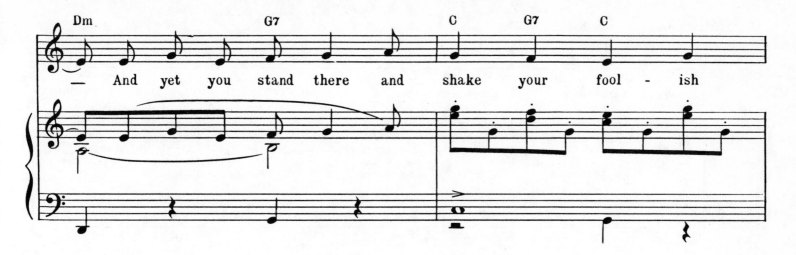

And yet you stand there and shake your fool - ish

head dra - ma - tic - 'lly. While I wait here

So ec - sta - tic - 'lly You just look and say em - pha - tic - 'lly

L'istesso tempo

Not this sea - son! There's a rea - son!

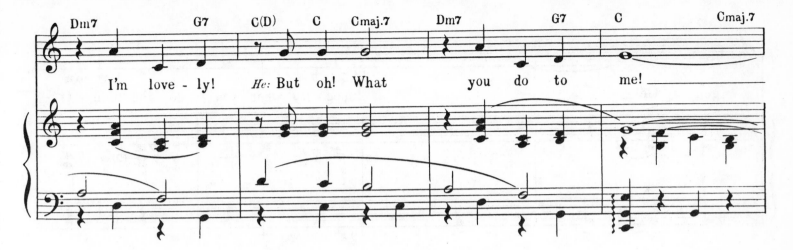

I'm love-ly! *He:* But oh! What you do to me!

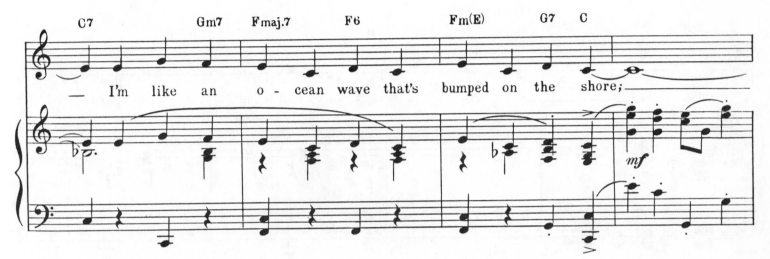

I'm like an o-cean wave that's bumped on the shore;

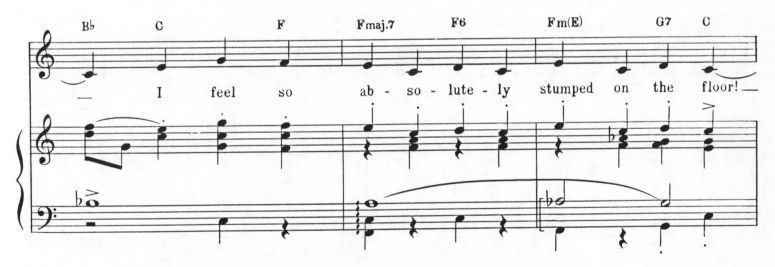

I feel so ab-so-lute-ly stumped on the floor!

She: When you dance you're charm-ing and you're

144

gen - tle!_____ 'Spec -'lly when you do the "Con - ti -

nen - tal."_____ *He:* But this feel - ing is - n't pure - ly

men - tal;_____ For heav - en rest us,_____ I'm not as -

bes - tos._____ And that's why I won't dance!

Why should I? I won't dance! How could I?

I won't dance! *Mer - ci beau - coup!* I know that

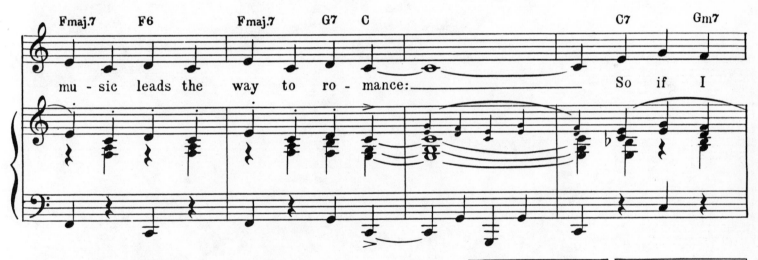

mu - sic leads the way to ro - mance: So if I

hold you in my arms I won't dance!

LAUGH AND LOVE DUO: RED SKELTON AND ANN MILLER PROVIDE LAUGHTER AS WELL AS ROMANCE IN "LOVELY TO LOOK AT."

From the MGM release "Lovely To Look At." © 1952 Loew's Incorporated

LOVELY TO LOOK AT. (Second Film Version) An M-G-M Picture (Technicolor) released in December, 1952. An adaptation of Roberta which starred Kathryn Grayson, Red Skelton, Howard Keel, Marge and Gower Champion, and Ann Miller. Produced by Jack Cummings [married to Kern's daughter, Betty, at the time]. Directed by Mervyn LeRoy and Vincente Minnelli.

LOVELY TO LOOK AT

Words by DOROTHY FIELDS & JIMMY McHUGH
Music by JEROME KERN

Refrain *(gracefully)*

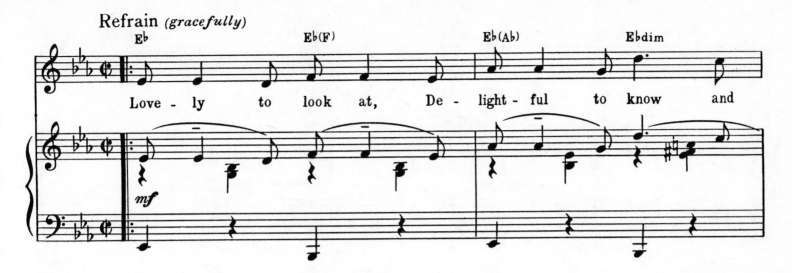

Love - ly to look at, De - light - ful to know and

heav - en to kiss._____ A com - bin -

a - tion like this,_____ Is quite my

most im - pos - si - ble scheme come true, Im - a - gine find - ing a dream like you! You're

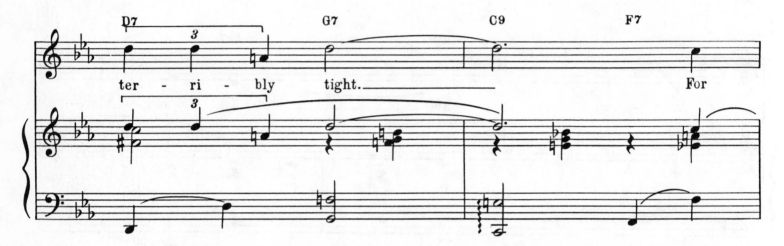

I DREAM TOO MUCH. An RKO Picture released in November, 1935. It starred Lily Pons and featured Henry Fonda, Eric Blore, Osgood Perkins [actor Anthony Perkins' father], Lucille Ball and Micha Auer. Lyrics by Dorothy Fields. Produced by Pandro S. Berman. Directed by John Cromwell.

LILY PONS HAS A HANDSOME ACCOMPANIST IN HENRY FONDA IN THE FILM "I DREAM TOO MUCH."

I DREAM TOO MUCH

Words by DOROTHY FIELDS
Music by JEROME KERN

155

And yet my dreams have shown____

Per - haps I dream____ too much a - lone.____

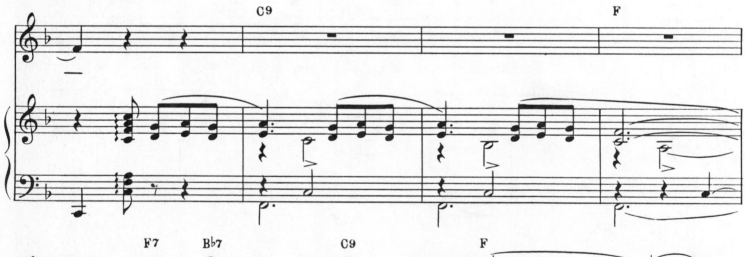

(Hums) Um-m-m-m Per-haps I dream too much a - lone.____

SWING TIME. An RKO Picture released in August, 1936. It starred Fred Astaire and Ginger Rogers and featured Helen Broderick and Victor Moore. Lyrics by Dorothy Fields. Produced by Pandro S. Berman. Directed by George Stevens.

Arthur Schwartz, the noted composer-producer has an amusing story about Kern and SWING TIME:

Jerry has played the piano for years, but with no particular flair. In fact, what he does to his own tunes at the piano is sheer murder. This is not helped by the fact that he never attempts to "put over" his songs. When he first played the score of SWING TIME for the RKO executives, there was silence. Stony, if not stricken, faces were all over the room. Yet, out of his score for that film came "The Way You Look Tonight," "A Fine Romance" and the bouncy "Pick Yourself Up."

"The Way You Look Tonight" won an Academy Award as the best song of 1936. Also included in the score, the exciting "Waltz In Swing Time."

GINGER ROGERS, AS SHE LOOKS AT FRED ASTAIRE, WONDERS IF THIS COULD BE "A FINE ROMANCE."

A FINE ROMANCE

Words by DOROTHY FIELDS
Music by JEROME KERN

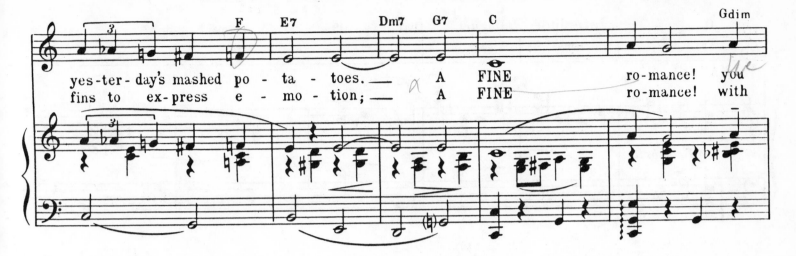

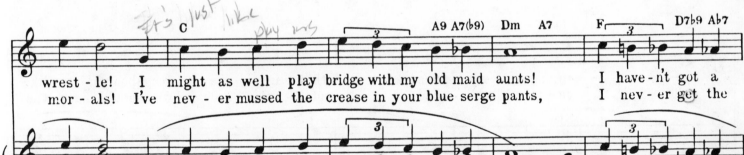

160

PICK YOURSELF UP

Words by DOROTHY FIELDS
Music by JEROME KERN

Start all o - ver a - gain. Don't lose your con - fi - dence

if you slip, be grate - ful for a pleas - ant trip, And

Pick your-self up, Dust your-self off, Start all o - ver a - gain.

Work like a soul in - spir - ed, Till the bat - tle of the day is won.

WALTZ IN SWING TIME

Words by DOROTHY FIELDS
Music by JEROME KERN

Pick your-self up,___ Dust your-self off,___ And then let's swing!

Poco meno mosso

Tempo I

THE WAY YOU LOOK TONIGHT

Words by DOROTHY FIELDS
Music by JEROME KERN

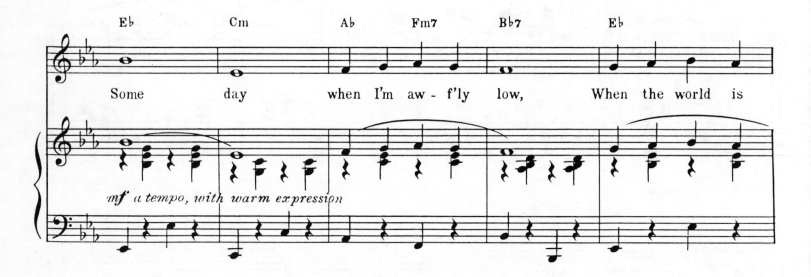

Some day when I'm aw-f'ly low, When the world is

cold, I will feel a glow just think-ing of you

And the way you look to - night.

Oh, but you're love - ly, With your smile so warm,

And your cheek so soft, There is noth-ing for me but to love

you, Just the way you look to - night.

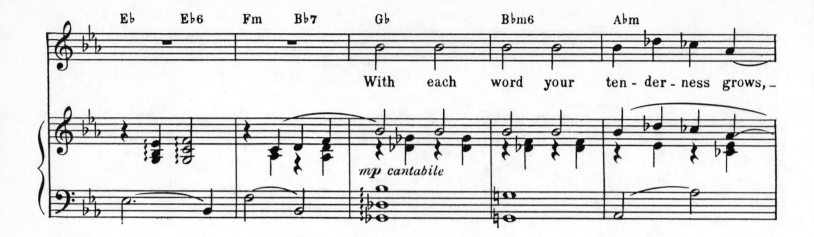

With each word your ten-der-ness grows,

Tear-ing my fear a - part,

And that laugh that wrink-les your nose Touch-es my

fool - ish heart. Love - ly,

never, nev-er change, Keep that breath-less charm, Won't you please ar-

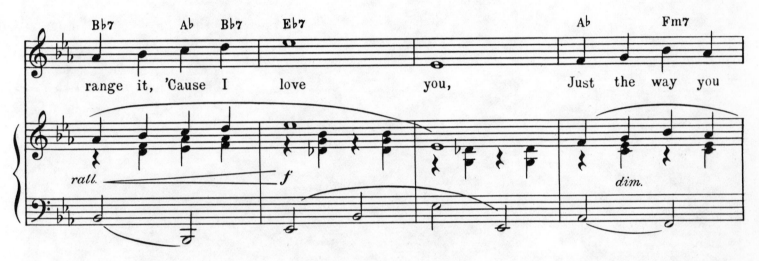

range it, 'Cause I love you, Just the way you

look to-night, mm— mm— mm—

mm— Just the way you look to-night.

HELEN BRODERICK AND GINGER ROGERS CONGRATULATE VICTOR MOORE AND FRED ASTAIRE ON
"THE WAY THEY LOOK TONIGHT."

HIGH, WIDE AND HANDSOME. A Paramount Picture released in May, 1937. It starred Irene Dunne and featured Randolph Scott, Dorothy Lamour, Elizabeth Patterson, Akim Tamiroff, Ben Blue, William Frawley and Alan Hale. Original Story, Screenplay and Lyrics by Oscar Hammerstein II. Produced by Arthur Hornblow Jr. Directed by Rouben Mamoulian.

CHARLES BICKFORD, IRENE DUNNE AND RANDOLPH SCOTT IN A DRAMATIC SCENE FROM
"HIGH, WIDE AND HANDSOME."

"The Folks Who Live On The Hill"
This is Kern in his loosest, most rhapsodic mood. There is enough melodic material in this piece for three different songs. Hammerstein's lyrics are pure and sentimental. He was always bothered by the obvious rhyme:
"Our veranda will command a . ."

THE FOLKS WHO LIVE ON THE HILL

Words by OSCAR HAMMERSTEIN II
Music by JEROME KERN

Man-y men with loft-y aims, Strive for loft-y

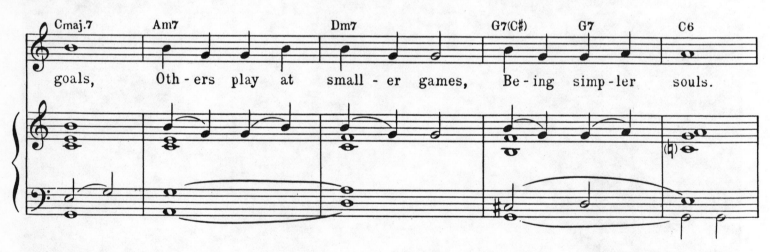

goals, Oth-ers play at small-er games, Be-ing simp-ler souls.

I am of the lat-ter brand; All I want to do Is to find a spot of land

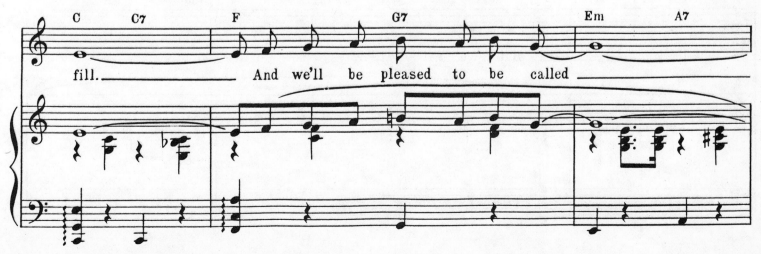

_"The folks who live on the hill!"

Some - day___ we may be add - ing a thing or two,___

a wing or two___ We will make chang - es as an - y fam' - ly

will,_____ But we will al - ways be called___

Just we two___ Dar - by and Joan— who used to be Jack— and

Jill, _____ The folks who like to be called _____ What they have al-ways been called

"The folks who live on the hill."___

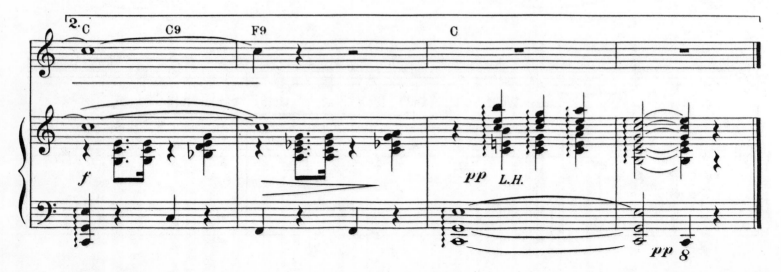

"Can I Forget You?"
This piece, with its naive, folksongish melody is rather like the songs of Stephen Foster.

IRENE DUNNE AND RANDOLPH SCOTT

CAN I FORGET YOU

Words by OSCAR HAMMERSTEIN II
Music by JEROME KERN

più cantabile ed espressivo

Will the glo - ry of your near - ness fade, As

moon - light fades in a veil of rain? Can I for -

get you, When ev - 'ry night re - minds me How much I want you back a -

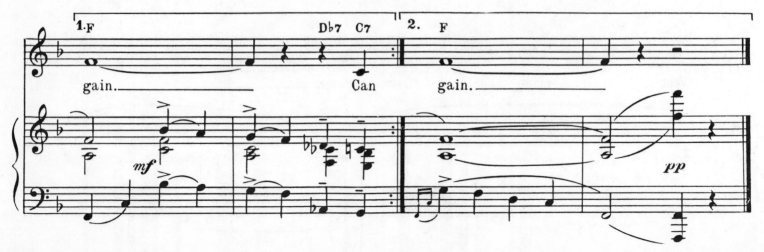

gain._____ Can gain._____

JOY OF LIVING. An RKO Picture released in May, 1938. Starred Irene Dunne and featured Douglas Fairbanks Jr., Alice Brady, Guy Kibbe and Lucille Ball. Lyrics by Dorothy Fields. Directed by Tay Garnett.

This film marked the sixth appearance for Irene Dunne in a Kern musical. In 1927 she understudied the role of Magnolia in the Broadway production of

SHOW BOAT. When the National Company arrived in Los Angeles, with Miss Dunne now in the leading part, she was grabbed by the Hollywood studios. Her roles in Kern filmusicals were: ROBERTA (1935); SWEET ADELINE (1935); SHOW BOAT (1936); HIGH, WIDE AND HANDSOME (1937); and JOY OF LIVING (1938).

A POSTER FOR "THE JOY OF LIVING" SHOWING LUCILLE BALL IN ONE OF HER EARLIEST ROLES.

When I first heard "You Couldn't Be Cuter" I wouldn't believe that it had been written by Kern. It bears none of his characteristics. But that has no validity if you remember that he also wrote that sexy-vamp, "I'll Be Hot to Handle" for the musical ROBERTA.

As to the lyrics for this song: Dorothy Fields once told me that her son, David, then just an infant, inspired the title.

YOU COULDN'T BE CUTER

Words by DOROTHY FIELDS
Music by JEROME KERN

got me lit-tle fel-la, I'm sunk! I'm gone! I'm hooked!

Refrain-Moderately *(in intimate conversational style)*

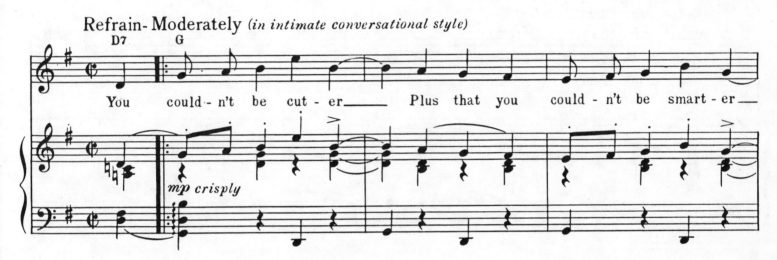

You could-n't be cut-er____ Plus that you could-n't be smart-er____

____ Plus that in-tel-i-gent face you have a dis-grace-ful

charm for me. You could-n't be keen-er, ____ you look so

fresh from the clean - er, ___ You are the lit - tle grand slam I'll

bring to my fam - i - ly. _____ My ma will show you an

al - bum of me that - 'll bore you to tears! _____ And

you'll at - tract all the rel - a - tives we have dodged for years and years. And

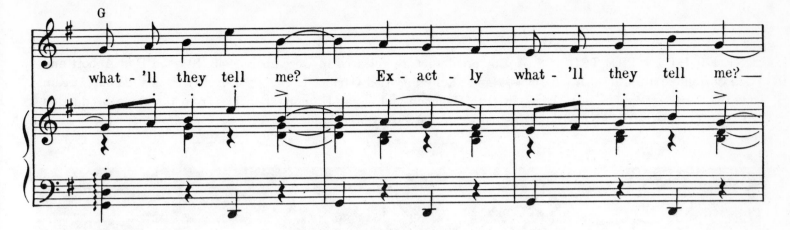

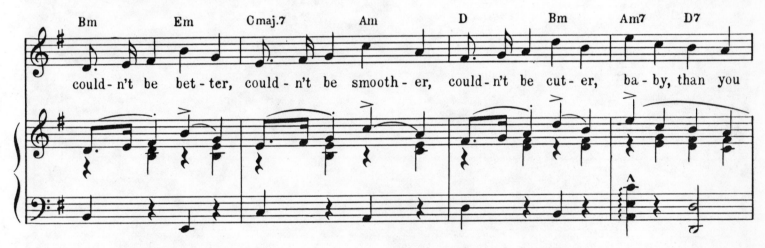

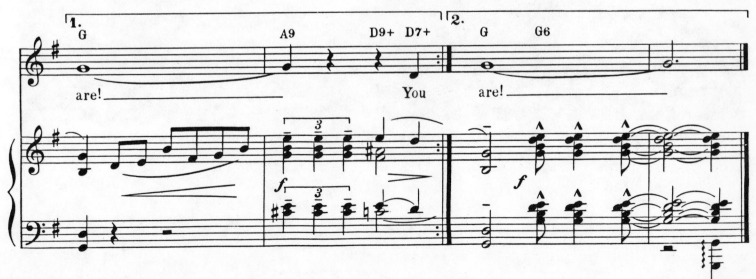

ONE NIGHT IN THE TROPICS. A Universal Picture released in December, 1940. Starred Bud Abbott and Lou Costello and featured Allan Jones, Nancy Kelly and Leo Carillo. Lyrics by Dorothy Fields. "Your Dream (Is the Same as My Dream)" lyrics by Otto Harbach and Oscar Hammerstein II (from the stage production of GENTLEMAN UNAFRAID). Directed by A. Edward Sutherland.

ROBERT CUMMINGS, NANCY KELLY (BACK ROW) SEEM TO OBJECT TO PEGGY MORAN'S HEAD ON ALLAN JONES' SHOULDER.

REMIND ME

Words by DOROTHY FIELDS
Music by JEROME KERN

Re - mind me

— not to find you so at-trac - tive, ___ Re - mind me ___

— That the world is full of men, ___ When I start to

miss you, To touch your hand, To kiss you, Re -

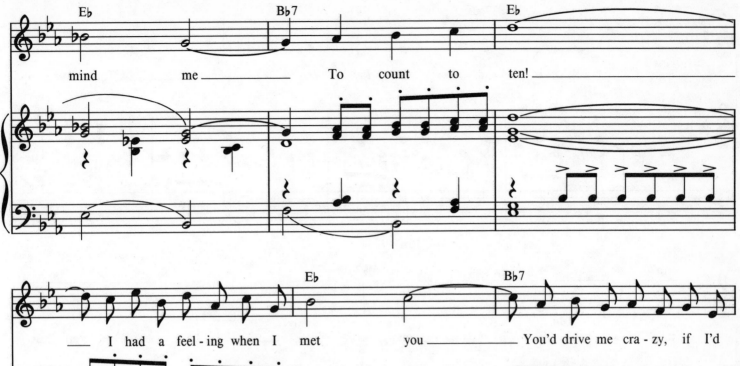

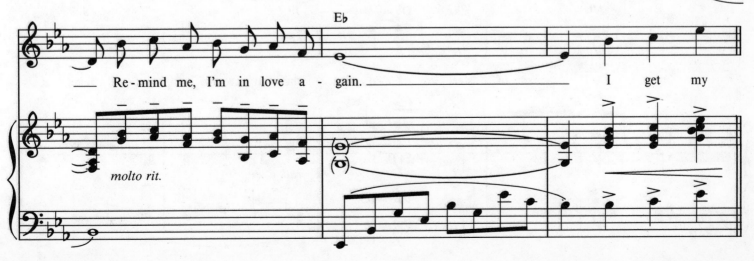

Poco animato *(alla Rhumba)*

heart well in hand, and I'm cer - tain, _____ That I can

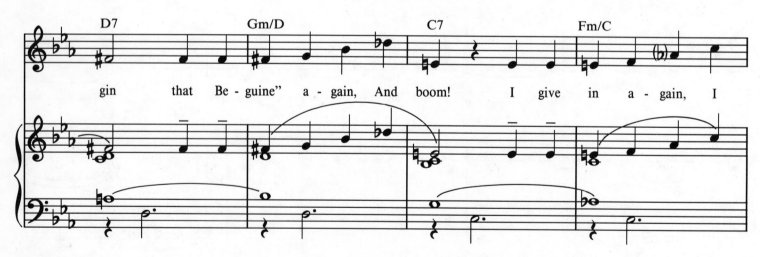

take you or leave you a - lone, _____ Then you "Be -

gin that Be - guine" a - gain, And boom! I give in a - gain, I

have a will _ made of steel my friend, But when it seems a - bout to bend, Re -

Slow Rhumba *(seductively)*

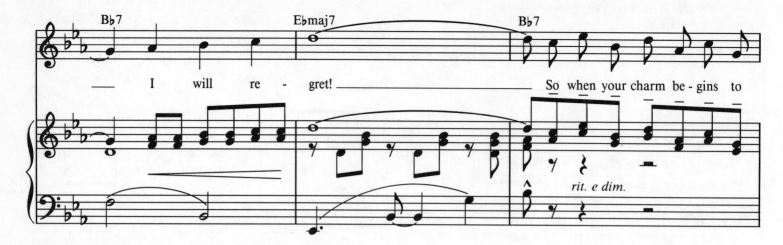

I will re- gret! _____ So when your charm be- gins to

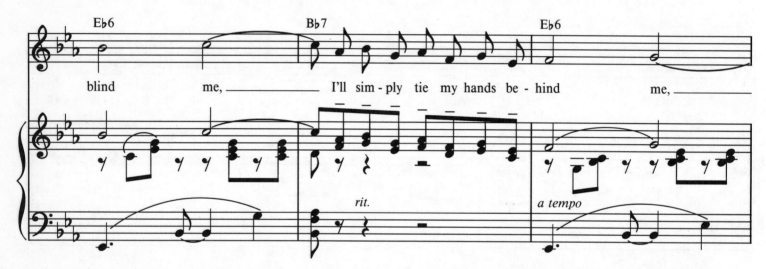

blind me, _____ I'll sim- ply tie my hands be- hind me, _____

Don't let me kiss you, please re- mind me, _____ Un- less, my dar- ling you for-

get. _____

LADY BE GOOD. A Metro-Goldwyn-Mayer Picture released in May, 1941. Cast included Ann Sothern, Eleanor Powell, Robert Young and Lionel Barrymore. Songs by George and Ira Gershwin, Arthur Freed and Roger Edens, and Jerome Kern and Oscar Hammerstein II. Musical Numbers staged by Busby Berkeley. Musical Director Georgie Stoll. Orchestrations by Conrad Salinger and Leo Arnaud. Associate Producer Roger Edens. Directed by Norman McLeod. Produced by Arthur Freed.

"The Last Time I Saw Paris" was not written for LADY BE GOOD nor any other motion picture or stage play. Messrs. Kern and Hammerstein just allowed Arthur Freed to use it in his filmusical.

Hammerstein tells about how the song came to be written:

This was the only song that I've ever written under any kind of compulsion. The Germans had just taken Paris and I couldn't get my mind on anything else at all. I loved the city very much and I hated the idea of it falling. I thought of the enemy tramping through the streets and taking all the gaiety and beauty out of the hearts of the people there. I thought of Mistinguette and her vastly insured legs and her shock of hair that she would shake when she sang. I thought of Chevalier with his straw hat. And, not just the beauty of the parks or the loveliness in the museums but everything that was Paris: good and bad and of high quality and of cheapness. And this was kind of a lament.

When I called Jerry and asked him to write some music for it, he almost fell dead. In all the years we'd been working together, this was the first time I had completed a lyric that he would have to set to music. He always wrote the melody and then I would fit words to it.

Kern took the words down over the telephone and three days later, when Hammerstein arrived on the coast, he was handed the finished manuscript.

Incidentally, both men were quite upset upon receiving news that "The Last Time I Saw Paris" had won an Academy Award. To be sure, they were pleased that the song was such a success, but, it had not been written for a motion picture. Kern saw to it that the Academy changed its rules making only those songs expressly written for a film eligible for an Oscar.

From The MGM Release "Lady Be Good" © 1941 Loew's Incorporated Copyright Renewed 1968 by Metro-Goldwyn-Mayer, Inc.

ALL-STAR CAST, RED SKELTON, ELEANOR POWELL, ROBERT YOUNG, AND JOHN CARROLL WITH ANN SOTHERN, WHO INTRODUCED THE ACADEMY-AWARD WINNING SONG IN THIS PICTURE.

THE LAST TIME I SAW PARIS

Words by OSCAR HAMMERSTEIN II
Music by JEROME KERN

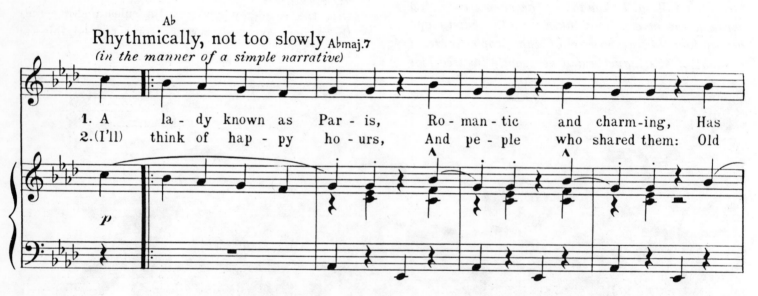

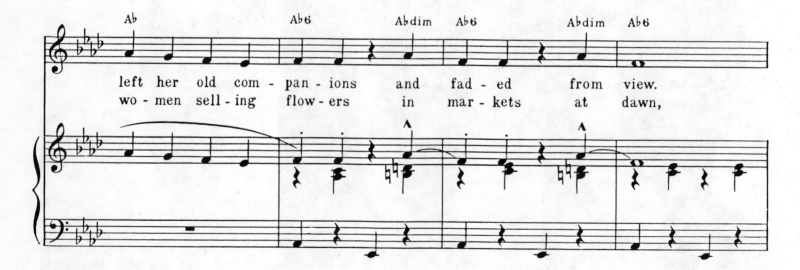

fé. The last time I saw Par - is, Her trees were dressed for

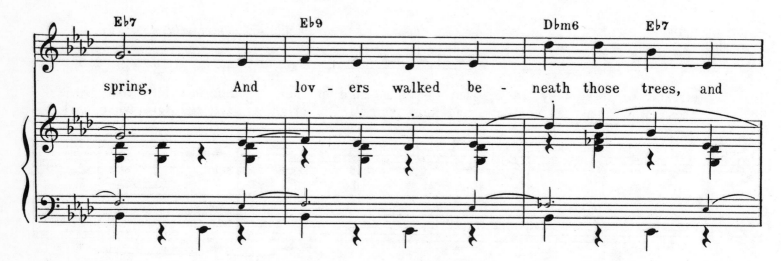

spring, And lov - ers walked be - neath those trees, and

birds found songs to sing. I dodged the same old tax - i - cabs that

I had dodged for years; The cho - rus of their

squeak-y horns was mu-sic to my ears. The last time I saw

Par-is, Her heart was warm and gay. No mat-ter how they

change her, I'll re-mem-ber her ___ that way.

2. I'll way. ___

YOU WERE NEVER LOVELIER. A Columbia Picture (Technicolor) released in December, 1942. Starred Fred Astaire and Rita Hayworth and featured Adolphe Menjou. Lyrics by Johnny Mercer. Directed by William A. Seiter.

Fred Astaire, in his autobiography STEPS IN TIME, describes the rehearsals on this film:

Rita and I had a romantic type dance to the song "You Were Never Lovelier." Keeping the laughs going during the intervals was a part of the day's work and I always tried to think up some gag to play on Rita. In one instance I called out, "well — here we go — I'm beginning to like this place — it doesn't get me down anymore, I'm used to it — ready, Rita?"

Up jumped Rita at once and came to me to start our first step together. As I took hold of her two arms she let out one scream and backed away. I had just dipped both my hands and arms in a bucket of ice which we kept for Coca-Cola bottles. That broke up rehearsals for an hour or so.

THE DEBONAIR ADOLPHE MENJOU, THE SULTRY MISS RITA HAYWORTH AND THE FASTEST-FEET IN THE WEST, FRED ASTAIRE.

DEARLY BELOVED

Words by JOHNNY MERCER
Music by JEROME KERN

Refrain-Andante cantabile, ma ben ritmato

Dear - ly be - lov - ed, how clear - ly I see,

Some - where in Heav - en you were fash - ioned for me,

An - gel eyes _____ knew you, _____

An - gel voi - ces led me to you; _____

Noth - ing could save me, Fate gave me a sign;

I know that I'll be yours come show - er or shine;

So I say _____ mere - ly, _____ Dear - ly be-

lov - ed be mine.   mine. _____

I'M OLD FASHIONED

Words by JOHNNY MERCER
Music by JEROME KERN

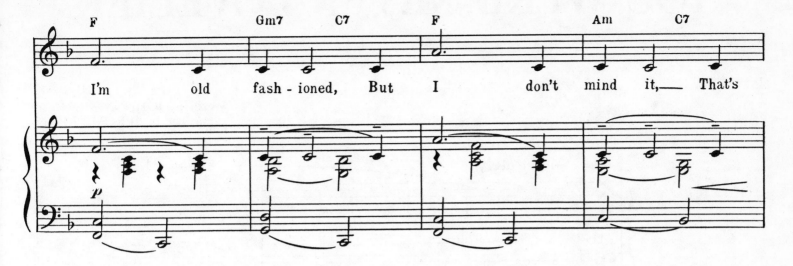

I'm old fash - ioned, But I don't mind it,___ That's

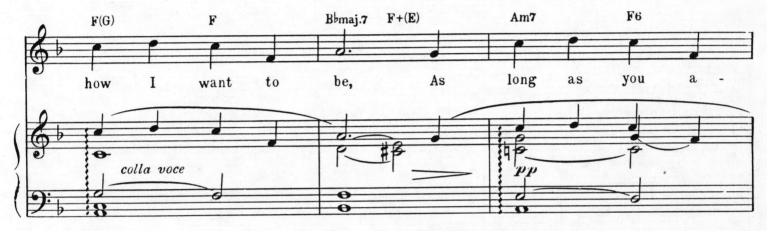

how I want to be, As long as you a -

gree to stay, old fash - ioned with

me.

me.___

YOU WERE NEVER LOVELIER

Words by JOHNNY MERCER
Music by JEROME KERN

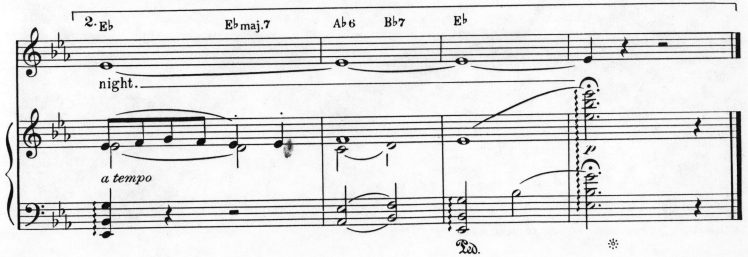

CAN'T HELP SINGING. A Universal Picture (Technicolor) released in December, 1944. Starred Deanna Durbin and featured Robert Paige, David Bruce and Akim Tamiroff. Lyrics by E. Y. Harburg. Produced by Felix Jackson. Directed by Frank Ryan.

FOR OPENERS, I THINK THE TITLE OF THIS FILM IS MORE DESCRIPTIVE OF DEANNA DURBIN THAN HER VEHICLE. KIDDING ASIDE, KERN WAS ONCE AGAIN AT HOME WITH A PERIOD PIECE: THE FIRST CALIFORNIA SETTLERS.

From the film "Can't Help Singing" Courtesy of Universal Pictures

CAN'T HELP SINGING

Words by E. Y. HARBURG
Music by JEROME KERN

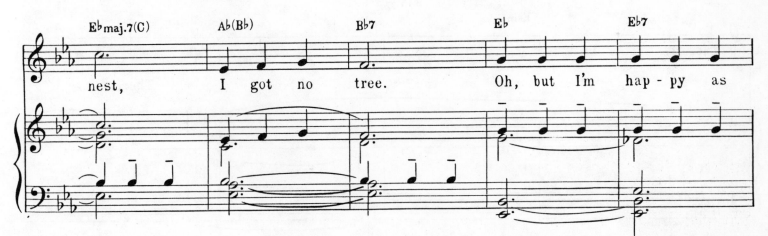

Refrain *(in bright waltz tempo)*

Can't help sing-ing _____ of a prom-ise that A-pril is bring-ing, _____ I am

float-ing a-long on the crest of a song, There are

bells in my heart and they're ring-ing. _____

COVER GIRL. A Columbia Picture (Technicolor) released in March, 1944. Starred Rita Hayworth and Gene Kelly and featured Phil Silvers, Lee Bowman, Jinx Falkenburg, Otto Kruger and Eve Arden. Lyrics by Ira Gershwin. Produced by Arthur Schwartz. Directed by Charles Vidor. Musical Director Morris Stoloff. Musical Supervisor Saul Chaplin. Orchestration by Conrad Salinger and Paul Weston.

THE CURBSTONE KIDS: GENE KELLY, RITA HAYWORTH AND PHIL SILVERS DANCING ON A BROOKLYN SIDEWALK.

From the Columbia Picture "Cover Girl" ©D-194-191

"Sure Thing"

Ira Gershwin, in his book LYRICS ON SEVERAL OCCASIONS, speaks about his work with Kern:

It was in 1939 that Kern was between assignments and I wrote nine or ten songs with him. Nothing ever happened to them although both of us liked several. During this time he played me many other tunes I liked but just didn't get around to. Some four years later, COVER GIRL period, I tried to remind him of a lovely tune of the earlier period by humming a snatch of it. But he had never put it on paper, and couldn't recall it. I told him his daughter Betty had been very fond of this melody, so he called her in and between us and our snatches, it came to him. "Good tune," he said. "What about it?" I told him it had begun haunting me that morning, and if he could split the opening note into two notes, I had a two-word on-the-nose title for the flashback number in the film — one which had a production idea for the choreographer and the designer. When he heard the title, "Sure Thing," with its race-track backgound, [Kern was an avid racing enthusiast] he said: "Of course — nothing to it — in fact, the two notes make a better announcement."

LONG AGO (AND FAR AWAY)

Words by IRA GERSHWIN
Music by JEROME KERN

Drear - y days are o - ver. Life's a four - leaf clo - ver.

Ses - sions of de - pres - sions are through _____ Ev - 'ry

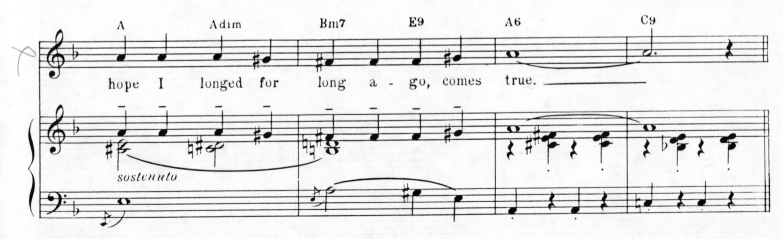

hope I longed for long a - go, comes true. _____

Refrain *(cantabile)*

Long a - go and far a - way, I dreamed a dream one

day And now that dream is here be - side me.

Long the skies were o - ver - cast, But now the clouds have

passed: You're here at last! _____ Chills run

up and down my spine, A - lad - din's lamp is mine, The dream I

dreamed was not de - nied me. Just one look and then I

knew _____ That all I longed for long a - go, was

1. you.

2. you. _____

SURE THING

Words by IRA GERSHWIN
Music by JEROME KERN

The fav-o-rite does-n't al-ways win, No mat-ter what the odds. Since no-bod-y knows how they'll come in, I leave it to the gods. So

CORNELL WILDE USES HIS CHARM ON LINDA DARNELL, RIGHT, AS JEANNE CRAIN DISAPPROVES IN "CENTENNIAL SUMMER."

CENTENNIAL SUMMER. A Twentieth Century-Fox Film (Technicolor) released in July, 1946. Starred Jeanne Crain, Cornell Wilde, Linda Darnell, William Eythe, Walter Brennan, Constance Bennett and Dorothy Gish. Lyrics by Leo Robin, E. Y. Harburg, Johnny Mercer and Oscar Hammerstein II. Musical Director Alfred Newman. Orchestrations by Conrad Salinger, Edward Powell, Earl Hagen and Maurice DePackh. Produced and Directed by Otto Preminger.

In 1945, Metro-Goldwyn-Mayer released their exciting new musical, MEET ME IN ST. LOUIS, which centered around the famous fair of 1906 in that city. The story also made overtures to the already legendary LIFE WITH FATHER.

As was Twentieth Century-Fox's wont, they promptly announced their forthcoming CENTENNIAL SUMMER dealing with a family in 1876 Philadelphia at the time of the Exposition.

Although this old-fashioned tale was ideally suited for Kern's magical touch, this his 109th and final score, presented problems. The cast was made up of non-singers. Otto Preminger, the film's producer and director was not what you would call an expert when it comes to musical production. But, most of all, Kern had a difficult time with his collaborator Leo Robin. "I was completely in awe of Kern from the minute we got together," says Robin, "and it cramped my style a little bit. He used to call me up every day, bugging me: 'You got anything yet?' I wanted so much to please him and to measure up to his high standard that I don't think I did my best work on that picture."

Kern became increasingly anxious as the weeks progressed until he finally had to call "Yip" Harburg, Johnny Mercer and Oscar Hammerstein 2nd to each do a song. Robin did complete two on his own: "Up With A Lark" and "In Love In Vain."

IN LOVE IN VAIN

Words by LEO ROBIN
Music by JEROME KERN

Moderato (whimsically)

Love can be a bless - ing, But al - so most de - press - ing, And I don't mind con - fess - ing That I feel might - y blue! It's on - ly hu - man for an - y - one to

Burthen, Slowly, lyrically

want to be in love, But who wants to be in love in

vain? _____ At night you hang a - round the house and eat your

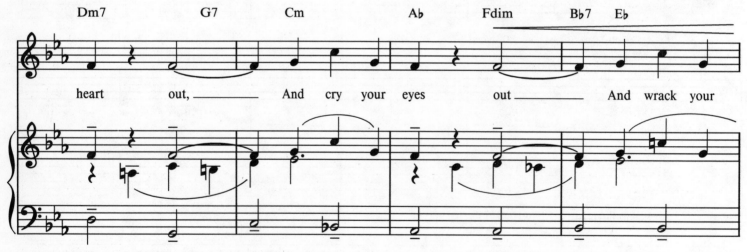

heart out, _____ And cry your eyes out _____ And wrack your

brain. _____ You sit and won - der why an - y - one as

ALL THROUGH THE DAY

Words by OSCAR HAMMERSTEIN II
Music by JEROME KERN

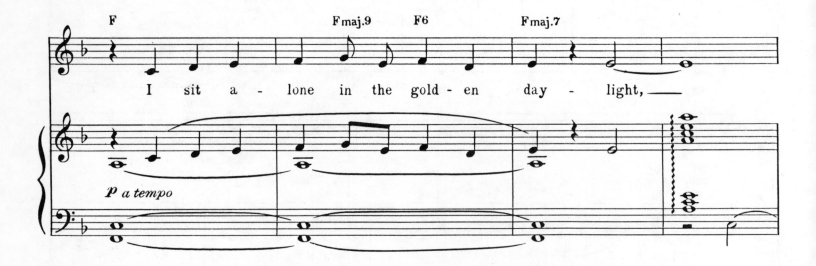

I sit a - lone in the gold - en day - light, ___

But all I see is a sil - ver sky; ___ For in my

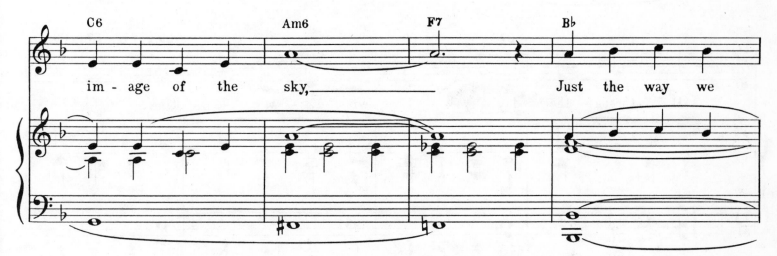

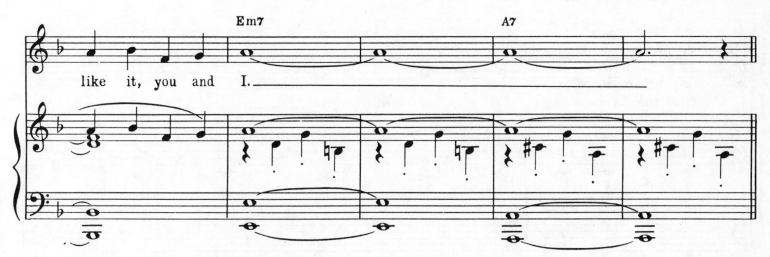

Refrain-Moderato *(lyrically)*

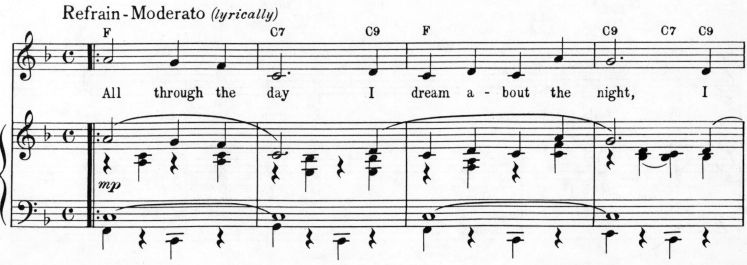

dream a-bout the night, Here with you.

All through the day I wish a-way the time, Un-

til the time when I'm here with you.

with great breadth

Down falls the sun, I run to meet you,

The eve-ning mist melts a-way;

Down smiles the moon, And soon your lips re-call The

kiss I dreamed of All through the day.

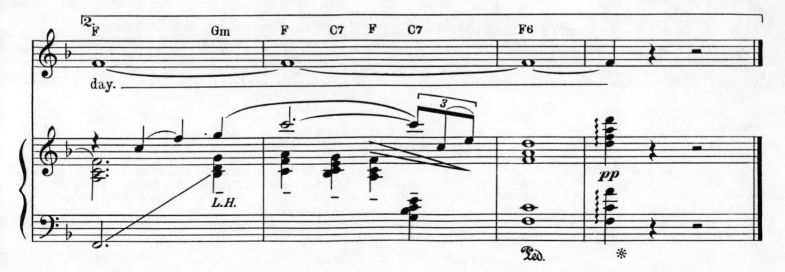

day.

Presidential Documents

Federal Register
Vol. 50, No. 18
Monday, January 28, 1985

Title 3—

The President

Proclamation 5293 of January 23, 1985

National Jerome Kern Day, 1985

By the President of the United States of America

A Proclamation

Musical theater is an American art form that has been part of our lives for over a century. The songs are a true expression of the era in which they were written, but they also evoke something eternal in the American ethos—echoing our joy in good years, reflecting our sadness in difficult ones, and lifting our spirits in times of challenge.

Jerome D. Kern, one of the founding fathers of the American musical theater, whose centenary we observe this year, is widely honored for his many contributions to this uniquely American art form. His prodigious body of work—over 1,000 songs and 108 complete scores for Broadway shows and Hollywood films—forms a major part of the core of musical theater as we know it in America and as it has spread throughout the world.

Jerome Kern is remembered for individual songs, such as "Lovely to Look At," "They Didn't Believe Me," "All the Things You Are," and "Look for the Silver Lining," as well as entire film and stage scores, most notably the classic *Show Boat*.

He collaborated with other great talents like Oscar Hammerstein II, Johnny Mercer, and Ira Gershwin and wrote with the elegance, wit, and sophistication that characterize the best American popular music. He was esteemed by his peers, who twice voted to honor him with Academy Awards—for "The Way You Look Tonight" and "The Last Time I Saw Paris." New generations of audiences of all ages and backgrounds have taken his melodies to heart and given them a permanent place in our American musical heritage.

In recognition of the many contributions of Jerome Kern in enriching the American musical theater and in celebration of the one hundredth anniversary of his birth, the Congress, by House Joint Resolution 583, has designated January 27, 1985, as "National Jerome Kern Day."

NOW, THEREFORE, I, RONALD REAGAN, President of the United States of America, do hereby proclaim January 27, 1985, as National Jerome Kern Day. I encourage the people of the United States to observe the day with appropriate ceremonies, programs, and activities throughout the country, and in particular, by enjoying the music of this renowned American composer.

IN WITNESS WHEREOF, I have hereunto set my hand this twenty-third day of January, in the year of our Lord nineteen hundred and eighty-five, and of the Independence of the United States of America the two hundred and ninth.

Ronald Reagan

[FR Doc. 85-2180
Filed 1-24-85; 12:42 pm]
Billing code 3195-01-M

Throughout 1985, the world lit up in celebration of the Centenary of the birth of Jerome Kern. This celebration, orchestrated by The Welk Music Group—publishers of the entire body of Kern's works—honored the composer in the world's top magazines and newspapers, revivals of many of his stage productions, retrospectives of his motion pictures, scholarly reviews of his compositions, cabaret and concert remembrances of his genius, a successful production of a new show featuring his music in London's prestigious West End, and the releases of hundreds of new and existing records to an audience eager to discover or rediscover America's own brand of classical music, invented by Kern. President Ronald Regan proclaimed January 27, 1985, "National Jerome Kern Day," and the United States Postal Service recognized Kern's unique place in American musical history with the issuance of a stamp commemorating his birth.

1985 reinforced, once again, the timelessness Kern's vision brought to the music he created; it opened the door to new generations who will marvel at the genius who produced music that will be revered as long as music exists.

My Friend....JEROME KERN *
by Oscar Hammerstein II

I have promised myself not to play upon your emotions—or on mine. We, in this chapel, are Jerry's "family." We all know him very well. Each of us knows what the other has lost.

I think he would have liked me to say a few words about him. I think he would not have liked me to offer feeble bromides of consolation—butterfly wings of trite condolence to beat against the solid wall of our grief. He would have known our grief was real, and must be faced.

On the other hand, I think Jerry would have liked me to remind you that today's mourning and last week's vigil will soon recede from our memories, in favor of the bright recollections of him that belong to us.

At the moment, Jerry is playing "out of character." The masque of tragedy was never intended for him. His death yesterday and this reluctant epilogue will soon be refocused into their properly remote place in the picture. This episode will soon seem to us to be nothing more than a fantastic and dream-like intrusion on the gay reality that was Jerry's life.

His gayety is what we will remember most— the times he has made us laugh; the even greater fun of making him laugh. It's a strange adjective to apply to a man, but you'll understand what I mean: Jerry was "cute." He was alert and alive. He "bounced." He stimulated everyone. He annoyed some. never bored anyone at any time. There was a sharp edge to everything he thought or said.

...We all know in our hearts that these few minutes we devote to him now are small drops in the ocean of our affections. Our real tribute will be paid over many years of remembering, of telling good stories about him, and thinking about him when we are by ourselves.

We, in this chapel, will cherish our special knowledge of this world figure. We will remember a jaunty, happy man whose sixty years were crowded with success and fun and love. Let us thank whatever God we believe in that we shared some part of the good, bright life Jerry led on this earth.

*(Eulogy delivered by Mr. Hammerstein at the funeral services)